First World War
and Army of Occupation
War Diary
France, Belgium and Germany

46 DIVISION
Headquarters, Branches and Services
Royal Army Veterinary Corps
Assistant Director Veterinary Services
3 September 1914 - 31 March 1919

WO95/2672/3

The Naval & Military Press Ltd
www.nmarchive.com
Published in association with The National Archives

Published by

The Naval & Military Press Ltd

Unit 10 Ridgewood Industrial Park,

Uckfield, East Sussex,

TN22 5QE England

Tel: +44 (0) 1825 749494

www.naval-military-press.com

www.nmarchive.com

This diary has been reprinted in facsimile from the original. Any imperfections are inevitably reproduced and the quality may fall short of modern type and cartographic standards.

© **Crown Copyright**
Images reproduced by permission of The National Archives, London, England, 2015.

Contents

Document type	Place/Title	Date From	Date To
Heading	WO95/2672/3 Assistant Director Veterinary Services.		
Miscellaneous			
War Diary	Diary		
Miscellaneous	Subject-War Diaries. W.M.D. 142/G.	22/09/1914	22/09/1914
Miscellaneous	War Diaries.	20/09/1914	20/09/1914
Miscellaneous	Skeleton Form Of War Diary.		
Heading	War Diary September 1914		
Miscellaneous		08/10/1914	08/10/1914
War Diary		03/09/1914	14/09/1914
Miscellaneous		08/10/1914	08/10/1914
Heading	War Diary September 1914		
Miscellaneous	(1) Veterinary Department.	06/11/1914	06/11/1914
Heading	War Diary October 1914		
War Diary	Luton	03/10/1914	25/10/1914
Miscellaneous	(1) Veterinary Department.	06/11/1914	06/11/1914
Heading	War Diary (November 1914) Lieut Colonel W.A. McDougall N. Mid. Division		
Miscellaneous	(1) Veterinary Department.	09/12/1914	09/12/1914
Miscellaneous			
War Diary	Luton	02/11/1914	08/11/1914
War Diary	Hertford	16/11/1914	16/11/1914
War Diary	Bishops Stfd	17/11/1914	30/11/1914
Miscellaneous	(1) Veterinary Department	09/12/1914	09/12/1914
Miscellaneous			
Heading	War Diary (December 1914) Lt. Colonel W.A. McDougall A.D.L.S. N. Mid. Division		
Miscellaneous	Statements For War Diary December 1914		
Miscellaneous	Skeleton Form Of War Diary.		
Miscellaneous	?Beilcops Startford.		
Miscellaneous	Statement For War Diary December 1914		
Miscellaneous	Skeleton Form Of War Diary.		
Miscellaneous	Headquarters. A.D.V.S.	29/12/1914	29/12/1914
Miscellaneous			
Miscellaneous	Statements For War Diary, January 1915	08/02/1915	08/02/1915
Miscellaneous	Bishops Stortford	01/01/1915	01/01/1915
Miscellaneous	To War Diary For February.		
Heading	46th Division A.D.V.S. 46th Division. Vol I 1-3-31-By 15 Vol.		
Heading	War Diary Lt. Colonel W.A. McDougall. A.D.M.S. 46th (North Midland) Division. From 1st March 1915 To 31st July 1915 Volume I		
Heading	46th Division. A.D.V.S. 46th Division Vol I 1-3-31-7-15 May		
Heading	War Diary Lt. Colonel Wauwbougal A.D.M.S. 46th (North Midland) Division. T.F. From 1st March 1915 To 31st July 1915. Volume I		
Miscellaneous			
Heading	46th Division. War Diary of Lt. Colonel W.A.Mc Dougall A.D.V.S. 46th (North Midland) Division. T.F. From 1st August 1915 To 31st August 1915 Vol II		

Type	Description	Start	End
Heading	46th Division War Diary of Lt. Colonel W.A. Mcdougall A.D.V.S. 46th (North Midland) Division T.F. From 1st August 1915 to 31st August 1915. Vol. II		
War Diary		08/08/1915	28/08/1915
Heading	46th Division A.D.V.S. 46th Division Vol III Sept 15		
Heading	War Diary of Lt. Colonel A.D.V.S. 46th (North'd) Division. T.F. From 1st September To 30th September 1915		
Heading	46th Division. A.D.V.S. 46th Division Vol III Sept 15		
Heading	War Diary of Lt. Colonel A.D.V.S. 46th (North'd) Division. T.F. From 1 Sept. 1915 To 30th Sept 1915		
War Diary		03/09/1915	26/09/1915
Heading	46th Division War Diary Lt. Colonel A.D.V.S. 46th (North Midland) Division. From 1st October 1915 To 31st October 1915 Vol IV		
War Diary		03/10/1915	30/10/1915
Heading	War Diary Lt. Colonel A.D.V.S. 46th (N.Mid) Division. From 1st November To 30th November 1915 Volume V		
War Diary		01/11/1915	07/11/1915
War Diary	La Fosse	09/11/1915	18/11/1915
Heading	War Diary of Lt. Colonel A.D.V.S. 46th (N. Mid) Division. From 1st December 1915 To 31st December 1915 (Volume 6)		
War Diary		05/12/1915	28/12/1915
Heading	A.D.V.S. 46th Division. Jan. Vol VII		
Heading	War Diary of Lt. Colonel A.D.V.S. 46th (North Midland) Division. T.F. From 1st January 1916 To 31st January 1916 (Volume 7)		
Heading	A.D.V.S. 46th Division. Jan. Vol VII		
Heading	War Diary of Lt. Colonel W.A. McDougall A.D.V.S. 46th (North Midland) Division T.F. From 1st January 1916 To 31st January 1916 Volume 7		
War Diary		04/01/1916	29/01/1916
Heading	War Diary of Lt. Colonel W.A. McDougall A.D.V.S. 46th (North Midland) Division T.F. From 1st Feby 1916 To 29th February 1916 Volume 8		
War Diary	Pout Rewy	20/02/1916	29/02/1916
Heading	War Diary of Lt. Colonel W.A. McDougall A.D.V.S. 46th (North Midland) Division T. From 1st March 1916 To 31st March 1916 Volume 9		
War Diary		03/03/1916	28/03/1916
Heading	War Diary of Lt. Colonel W.A. McDougall A.D.V.S. 46th (N. Midland) Division From 1st April 1916 To 30th April 1916 Volume X		
War Diary		05/04/1916	22/05/1916
War Diary	Pas	01/06/1916	30/06/1916
Miscellaneous	Headquarters 46th Division. Vol 13	05/08/1916	05/08/1916
War Diary	Pas	02/07/1916	03/07/1916
War Diary	Bavincourt	04/07/1916	31/07/1916
Miscellaneous	Memorandum. ADMS, ADVS 46th Division.	28/07/1916	28/07/1916
Heading	A.D.V.S. 46th Division. Vol 14 Aug		
War Diary	Bavincourt	01/08/1916	31/08/1916
Heading	War Diary September 1916 A.D.V.S. 46th Div.		
War Diary	Bavincourt	01/09/1916	30/09/1916
Miscellaneous	Headquarters 46th Division.	03/11/1916	03/11/1916

War Diary	Bavincourt	01/10/1916	31/10/1916
Diagram etc	Mange Chart 46th Division.		
War Diary	Frohen Le-Grand	01/11/1916	06/11/1916
War Diary	St. Riquier	06/11/1916	30/11/1916
War Diary	Lucheux	01/12/1916	06/12/1916
War Diary	Henu	07/12/1916	20/02/1917
War Diary	Gouy-En Artois.	21/02/1917	23/02/1917
War Diary	Henu	01/03/1917	20/03/1917
War Diary	Couin	21/03/1917	28/03/1917
War Diary	Norrent Fontes	29/03/1917	12/04/1917
War Diary	Busnes	13/04/1917	16/04/1917
War Diary	Labuissiere	17/04/1917	19/04/1917
War Diary	Sains-En-Gohelle	20/04/1917	30/04/1917
Diagram etc	Cases of Mange transferred to Base Weekly During Year.		
Miscellaneous	Cases of Mange evacuated.		
War Diary	Sains-En-Gohelle	01/05/1917	03/07/1917
War Diary	Curton	04/07/1917	24/07/1917
War Diary	Sailly-La-Bourse	25/07/1917	19/01/1918
War Diary	La Beuvriere	23/01/1918	08/02/1918
War Diary	Bomy	09/02/1918	27/02/1918
War Diary	Bomy Fouquieres	03/03/1918	07/03/1918
War Diary	Fouquieres Les. Bethune	08/03/1918	12/03/1918
War Diary	Fouquieres	13/03/1918	31/03/1918
War Diary	Bracquemont	02/04/1918	09/04/1918
War Diary	Bruay	13/04/1918	20/04/1918
War Diary	Gosnay	24/04/1918	30/04/1918
Miscellaneous	List of limits attached to 46th Division in Lens Sector.		
War Diary	Gosnay	02/05/1918	29/05/1918
Miscellaneous	Special War Diary 46th. (North Midland) Division.	04/06/1918	04/06/1918
War Diary	Gosnay	01/06/1918	12/09/1918
War Diary	Beaucourt Sur L'Hallue	14/09/1918	17/09/1918
War Diary	Tertry	19/09/1918	20/09/1918
War Diary	Vraignes	21/09/1918	02/10/1918
War Diary	R.I.b.8.8. Vendelles	03/10/1918	09/10/1918
War Diary	Fresnoy	10/10/1918	30/10/1918
War Diary	Bohain	31/10/1918	03/11/1918
War Diary	Molain	05/11/1918	05/11/1918
War Diary	Catillon	06/11/1918	06/11/1918
War Diary	Prisches	08/11/1918	10/11/1918
War Diary	Sains Du Nord	11/11/1918	14/11/1918
War Diary	Landrecies	15/11/1918	09/01/1919
War Diary	Le Cateau	10/01/1919	31/03/1919

00951/2672/3
Assistant Director Veterinary Services

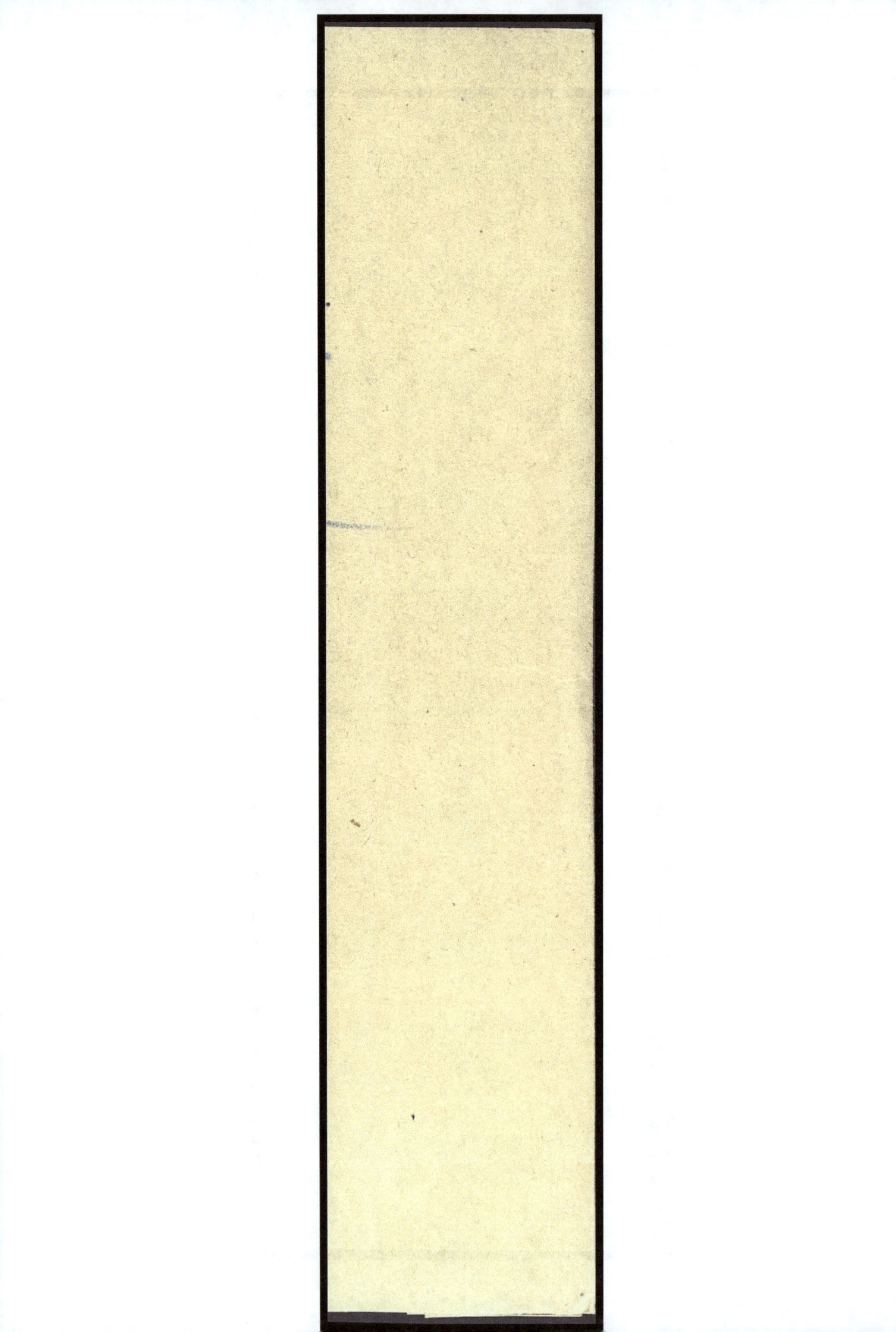

Diary

Lt. Colonel W. A. MacDougall A.D.V.S.
N. Mid. Div. T.F.

1914

3rd Aug! Lichfield — Notified all Officers A.V.C T.F. to their places by wire: Majors A. Waskin, & F. W. Allwood Rgde. & Nott & Derby Mounted Rgds. Also notified the O.C. the units. Roads were extolling to O.Cs with list except of the two Mounted Rgde T.F. lost had to be —

4th Aug! " — Wires to all officers A.V.C. asking if they were willing to embark on active foreign service. Obtained the sanction of the G.O.C. N. Mid. Div. — & Staff T.F. Officer to a list of recruiting for N. Mid. Div. Vety Hosp!. Wired Major T. H. Cox that he could begin recruiting.

5th Aug! — Left Head Station for temporary War Station (Derby). 10 Men recruited at Stoke on Trent for N. Mid. Vety Hosp!.

6th Aug! Derby — Selected site at Derby for Vety Hosp!. (Strettons Old Brewery)

7th " " — Recd. telegrams from W.O.Recd. urgent. Capt. H.B. Graham, Lieuts. H. T. Hadley, T. Thomson & T. Hagshaw to join our Refly. Force at once. These Officers left the same night. The cancel four vacancies for 6 Units of the Div.

8th " " — Engaged Mr. J. R. Crane as a C.V.S. & forwarded his application for a Special War Commn. in A.V.C. T.F. Engaged Mr. E. K. Nyland as a C.V.S. & forwarded his application for a Special War Commn. in A.V.C. T.F. Also Mr. A. Scotson. The management at all stations for Mob. Vety. Hosp!. as being filled with Uniform &c.

9th to 11th Aug! — Too busy to make any entries in diary

11th Aug! " — Abandoned Strettons old Brewery as a site for Vety Hosp!. as the Paddock Loose-boxes &c. at Derby Racecourse could now be obtained & Vety Hosp!. was established there

to
14th " — The A.V.C. personnel of N. Mid. Vety Hosp!. are gradually being supplied with uniform &c.

War Diary Cont'd

15th Augt	Derby	Went to Lichfield to see Regimental Paymaster about arrangements for paying the personnel of 6 Med. Cty. Hosp'l. Obtained the necessary information which I passed on to O.C. the Unit.
16th	"	Recce of the Unit. left Derby for Luton on 15th & today.
17th	"	left Derby for Luton with Lieut O.J. Rivers. Introduced A.D.O.S. to Comd'r at Derby before leaving. By order of O Comd'r all Cty. Ordnance Stores which were obtained for the 6 Med. Vety. Hosp'l. were left at Derby for the use of a new Vety Hosp'l. with a Civilian personnel.
18th	Luton	6 Med. Vety Hosp'l came to Luton from Derby but without any Vety or Ordnance Equipment so y't Vety Hosp'l. could not be opened at once at Luton.
19th to 25th Augt	"	Visited the V.O. at the various Units &c. & selecting of case for Vety Hosp'l. Fixed on the Cattle Shed, Stockwood Park, Luton. Strangles & Tetanus exist to a considerable extent in the Mounted Units. The cases are being dealt with & prophylactic measures &c.
27th	"	New Vety Hosp'l. opened in Stockwood Park. as Vety Equipment has been received but no Ordnance Stores have come to hand although every effort has been made.
30th	"	75 horses were rec'd from 1 Med. Mounted Bgde for treatment in Div'l Vety Hosp'l.
31st	"	Lieut J.R. Crane AVC T.F. reported him- self from Derby for duty & was posted to Div'l Vety Hosp'l.

Subject - War Diaries.   N.M.D. 142/G.

G̶.̶S̶.̶ adv̶s̶

          The attached circular memorandum is forwarded
for information and guidance.
          Diaries will again reach this office on the
10th of each month, and will be accompanied by a
statement as pro forma.
          Attention is directed to the last sentence
of para 3.

                         W.H.F. WEBER   Lieut.Colonel.
LUTON.   General Staff North Midland Div. T.F.
22nd September, 1914.

CENTRAL FORCE.

War Diaries

1. An examination of the War Diaries submitted on the 15th September, in accordance with Central Force Order No.84, of 3rd September, 1914, has shown that, in the great majority of cases, it would be impracticable to gather from them "information for future reference with a view to effecting improvements in the organization, education, training, equipment and administration of the Army for War" (Field Service Regulations, Part II (Para.140 I(ii).

2. The diaries, as originally ordered, will continue to be sent in on the 15th of each month. In addition, a statement (not in diary form), will be prepared by every unit of the Central Force, dealing specifically with the lessons gained from experience during the period of mobilization and subsequently.

3. This statement will be prepared monthly, and will accompany the diary. It will embody, as briefly as possible, the experience of the previous month. Such a statement will be prepared by all units for the period from the first day of mobilization up to 30th September and will accompany the diary due in this office on the 15th October.

4. Brigade Commanders will summarize, as briefly as possible, the conclusions arrived at by the units under them and will say whether they agree with those conclusions.

Similarly, Divisional and Army Commanders will summarize the conclusions of their subordinates, and will add an expression of their own opinion.

5.

5. The accompanying form is published as a guide for the preparation of these statements. It is not intended that unit commanders shall report on all the subjects indicated. They should confine their remarks to subjects where they have specific defects to draw attention to, or definite recommendations to make to improve matters.

The purpose of the Report, as stated in paragraph 1, must be constantly borne in mind.

Remarks under any heading should be as concise and as much to the point as possible.

Horse Guards,
 Whitehall, S.W.
  20th September, 1914.

C Ross Colonel
for Chief of General Staff
Central Force.

SKELETON FORM OF WAR DIARY

    Unit ....

    Brigade ....

    Division ....

    Mobilization Centre ....

    Temporary War Station ....

    Stations since occupied subsequent to Concentration :-

    ....

    ....

(a) <u>MOBILIZATION</u>

(b) <u>CONCENTRATION AT WAR STATIONS</u> (including Railway Moves)

(c) <u>ORGANIZATION FOR DEFENCE</u> (including vulnerable points)

(d) <u>TRAINING</u>

(e) <u>DISCIPLINE</u>

(f) <u>ADMINISTRATION</u>

    1. Medical Services

    2. Veterinary Services

    3. Supply Services

    4. Transport Services

    5. Ordnance Services

    6. Billeting and Hutting

    7. Channels of correspondence in routine matters

    8. Range construction

    9. Supply of Remounts

(g) <u>REORGANIZATION OF T.F. INTO HOME & IMPERIAL SERVICE</u>

(h) <u>PREPARATION OF UNITS FOR IMPERIAL SERVICE</u>

War Diary

(September) 1914

(Further Reminiscences)

An Outing for reminiscence & by O Howard which assembled
on 22nd Sept in

Stangles & Contagious Catarrh amongst the horses of the
Division is decreasing. The inquiry leads which have
amongst the first above effects being nearly free
from this disease. The Division Veterinary Hospital is doing
good work & has over 200 horses suffering from these diseases.

(H Colonel
A.D.V.S. for Lieut Col ADumours

Lt Col
ADumours

Diary for September
Lt-Col. MacDougall A.D.V.S. 6th Div.

Date	Place	Information	Remarks
2 Sept	Luton	A.A. Scott & 4 & 9 N.C.O.s, 1 Civilian Steering Smith & 21 Civilian Horsekeepers (and Veterinary & Ordnance Stores) arrived at Luton from Derby. The Reserve Vety Hospl. at Derby having been closed. Lieut Sabot was posted to 1 Med. Div. Vety. Hospl. for duty & the rest of the personnel attached to that Hospl. finding difficulty 12 of the Horsekeepers from Derby left of their own accord as they thought they were going to be supplied with Rations, Lodging &c in addition to their pay of 4/- a day. 2 Horsekeepers in addition to the 12 referred to above discharged. Leaving 7 Derby Horsekeepers with Div. Hosp.	
"	"	8 Railway Warrants was issued & the 12 Horsekeepers sent back to Derby.	
"	"	Inspected Sixth Lincolns. Northampton Yeo: 1st M.Md Bde R.F.A & 3rd M.Md Bde R.F.A. with A.D.V.S. 3rd Army. Also Div. Veterinary Hosp.	
"	"	Went to Luton H.Qrs to see A.D.V.S. 3rd Army about enlisting the Civilian Horsekeepers under Army Order (Special) 1 dated 4th Aug.t 1914. Have received instructions to enlist them under that Order & add names over the age laid down to be put forward for special authority.	

No Carbon paper between the Sheets here & owing to pressure of work I had not time to copy the entries here for the last half of month.

P.T.O.

(Attention Veterinary)

for meeting for reconsideration &, by a Board which assembled on 22nd Sept.

Sept 1914

Strangles & Contagious Catarrh amongst the horses of the Division is decreasing. The Mounted Units which were amongst the first to become affected being nearly free from these diseases. The Divisional Veterinary Hospital is doing good work, & has over 300 horses at present under treatment.

H H Dangar
Lt Colonel
A.D.V.S. North Md. Division

Seen
8/10/14

War Diary

(September) 1914

War Diary
October 1914

(1) Veterinary Department

(2) ----------

(3) North Midland Division

(4) Stoke on Trent for veterinary section

(5) Derby

(6) Luton

(a) Mobilization took place chiefly at Derby but several civilian veterinary Surgeons joined at Luton.

(b) Nil
(c) Nil
(d) The training of the personnel of the A.V.C. is purely technical practical ~~surgeon~~ experience is being gained daily

(e) Discipline is very good.
(f) Nil

2. The horsekeepers *a proportion* have now been enlisted so the difficulty mentioned is last statement has ~~now~~ been *partially* removed

3. Satisfactory

4. No information laid down in War Establishment as to number of waggons and carts for veterinary hospital

5. The Mobile *Veterinary* Section was satisfactorily equipped before leaving and the remainder is nearly so

6. Huts for men and sheds for horses are now approaching completion at Stockwood Park opposite to the present Hospital

7. Correspondence in some matters is very heavy

8. Nil

9. Remounts have now been supplied for the Hospital

G. All Officers except two and all the N.C.O's and men have volunteered for service abroad. One Mobile Section has already left for service abroad

H. ~~The Unit as a whole will~~ *A Second Mobile Veterinary Section is being* prepared for Imperial Service ~~by the time the Division is ordered to move~~, *& when the Stores are received will be ready — the personnel has been detailed.*

Town Hall

Luton

6/11/14

Lt Colonel
A.D.V.S. N.Mid Divn.

War Diary
October 1914

Copy   Diary for October.   Lt. Col. McDougall A.V.S. Veterinary

2nd Oct. Luton   Information was received from a private source that a case of mange had existed in the Stables of Messrs Hundrill & Andrell Road Luton a week before the yard in question was taken over by the 5th (Staffs) Regt. as a billet for their horses. I also learnt that two or three similar outbreaks had occurred in those stables within the last two years. The O.C. Staffs Infantry Brigade was informed & the horses were removed & picketted in the open where they were before brought in the stables. The V.O. i/c was instructed to inspect them daily.

4th Oct. "   A Casting Roll for fifty (50) horses was submitted for the approval of D.O.S. Between the 1st & 4th Oct. I visited the various Units & inspected the horses brought forward by the V.Os i/c for Casting for Veterinary Reasons. The majority of these horses were decrepit old & worn out, chronically lame &c: and ought never to have been bought. Judging from the state of those horses one cannot help forming the opinion that they must have been purchased without having first been submitted to a Veterinary examination.

8th " "   The Site for the Divl. Vety. Hospl. was decided on by the D.R.E. 3rd Army, & the position of the sheds &c; staked out. The site selected is a field on the other side of the London road from the present Hospital.

    Having heard that Farley Farm was only going to be occupied by the Remount Dept. for a short time, I represented to the D.D.S. 3rd Army the advisability of obtaining it for a Veterinary Hospital instead of the site selected. Over 200 horses could be put under cover at Farley Farm without adding to the existing buildings.

    The V.O. i/c R.E. Signal Companies at Houghton Regis received instructions to test with Mallein all the horses of those Companies as several cases of Glanders had occurred amongst them prior to their coming to Houghton Regis, & this work is gradually being carried out. Mange is said also to have existed in those Companies prior to their coming to Houghton Regis but no cases have occurred since

War Diary   Page 2

Date	Place	Information Lt Col McDougall	Remarks
14th to 20th Octr.	Luton	No. Mobile Veterinary Section in process of being formed from the personnel of the Divisional Veterinary Hospital. This Section left Luton on 20th Octr. under the command of Lieut O. H. Ryland AVC TF en route to Wantage to be attached to the 2nd South Midland Mounted Brigade. This Section named "B Mobile Veterinary Section" was to receive the Veterinary & Orange Equipment & Arms, Horses &c: at Wantage.	
22nd Oct.	"	Captain C Hartley AVC TF joined the Division from the 1st Mounted Division, to command a second Mobile Veterinary Section which is being formed. Lieut W.T Oliver AVC TF joined the 1st Mounted Division in exchange for Capt Hartley	
25th "	"	The new War Establishment for the Division came into force, and three Officers of the AVC TF are required to complete the AVC. Establishment for Imperial Service viz one for each of the following (1) Headquarters Staffordshire Infantry Brigade (2) " Notts & Derby Infantry Brigade (3) Divisional Ammunition Column	

R McDougall
Lt Colonel
ADVS North Midland Division

Luton
6th Novr 1914

Town Hall
Luton
6/11/14

Lt Colonel
A.D.V.S. N.M 1d Divn.

(1) Veterinary Department
(2) ---------
(3) North Midland Division
(4) Stoke on Trent for veterinary section
(5) Derby
(6) Luton

(a) Mobilization took place chiefly at Derby but several civilian Veterinary Surgeons joined at Luton.
(b) Nil
(c) Nil
(d) The training of the personnel of the A.V.C. is purely technical practical but much experience is being gained daily
(e) Discipline is very good.
(f) Nil (1) instruction

2 The horsekeepers have now been enlisted partially so the difficulty mentioned in last statement has now been removed

3. Satisfactory

4. No information laid down in War Establishment as to number of waggons and carts for veterinary hospital.

5. The Mobile Section was satisfactorily equipped before leaving *Artillery* and the remainder is nearly so

6. Huts for men and sheds for horses are now approaching completion at Stockwood Park opposite to the present Hospital

7. Correspondence in some matters is very heavy

8. Nil

9. Remounts have now been supplied for the Hospital

G. All Officers except two and all the N.C.O's and men have volunteered for service abroad. One Mobile Section has already left for service abroad

H. The Unit as a whole will a prepared for Imperial Service by the A civil Public Veterinary Duties is being

A *letter the State of are received will to right. to forward to* *been started.*

Copy

War Diary
(November 1914)

Lieut Colonel MacDougall
A.D.M.S.
N. Mid. Division.

Copy

War Diary
(November 1914)

Lieut-Colonel MacDougall
A.D.M.S.
N. Mid. Division

(1) Veterinary Department

(2) ---------------------

(3) North Midland Division

(4) Stoke on Trent for Veterinary Section.

(5) Derby

(6) Luton, Hertford, Bishops Stortford.

(a) Mobilization took place chiefly at Derby, but several civilian Veterinary Surgeons joined at Luton.

(b) Nil.

(c) Nil.

(d) The training of the personnel of the A.V.C. is chiefly technical. Practical experience is being gained daily.

(e) Discipline is very good.

(f) 1. Nil

2. As horsekeepers willing to serve abroad and to be enlisted are now to be employed at the Veterinary Hospital the difficulty of the civilian element has now been removed.

3. Satisfactory.

4. A suitable cart for the 2nd Mobile Section has yet to be obtained

5. The equipment of the Section is complete with the exception of arms and bandoliers

6. The sheds for the horses at London Road Luton, are now in use but more sheds are required to accomodate the whole of the horses. The huts for the men are at the present time not completely furnished.

7. Correspondence in some matters is very heavy

8. Nil

9. The establishment in remounts is complete. For the most part however they are too small for the purpose required.

(H) Two Veterinary Mobile Sections have already been prepared for Imperial Service

(G) All Officers except four and all the N.C.O's and men have volunteered for service abroad

MacDougall
Lt Colonel

Bishops Stortford
9/12/14

Cont'd

31st Nov Bishops Stfd. As a result these left in a body leaving Major Coe with a greatly increased number of horses, no veterinary help and a totally inadequate staff. Under the circumstances it is greatly to his credit that he has been able to carry on. So efficiently as has been the case.

DIARY FOR NOVEMBER   Lt. Colonel W.A.McDougall
                      A.D.V.S. N.Md. Division

Date	Place	Information	Remarks
2nd Nov.	Luton	Visited Hitchen to inspect the horses of the Yorkshire Hussars. Amongst them were about 20 mares in foal. As many of these are valuable animals a question of urgency arises as to what is the best thing to do with these mares, are they to be returned to a Remount Depot, or would it be advisable to let them out to farmers, etc, and after foaling, re-issue them to the Army.	
3rd "	"	Veterinary Officers were posted to units in accordance with the new War Office Establishments. Lieut A.J.Hines, who was in charge of Divl Headquarters was posted to the Staffs Infy Brigade in addition. Lieut J.A.Shaw, was posted to the Linc & Leics Infy Brigade. and Lieut A. Scotson was posted to the Divl Train. The C.F.order as to clipping, having appeared, a horse was clipped at the Veterinary Hospital, Stockwood Park, Luton, in accordance with the instructions contained therein, and inspected by the veterinary officers of the Division. The Clipping Machines not having arrived, however, no clipping could be done.	
6th "	"	The second Mobile Section is now in process of being formed under the command of Captain Chas Hartley.	
8th "	"	Major Johnson. A.V.C. reported himself at Luton for service with the North Midland Division. He was posted to the Notts & Derby Infantry Brigade at Harpenden.	
16th " 17th "	Hartford Bishops Stfd	The Division moved from Luton by route march to Hertford and on the 17th by route march to Bishops Stortford. Generally speaking the horses stood the journey well as the number of casualties reported was not excessive. It cannot be denied however that instances occurred of considerable overloading of horses thus causing undue distress. Probably the fact that several of the units were short of their establishment of horses and particularly draught horses rendered this overloading unavoidable but it accounts for a great number of the casualties which occurred. A number of horses which should undoubtedly have been left at the Veterinary Hospital, Stockwood Park, were also brought on the march and have since had to be returned by train to Luton. The second Mobile Veterinary Section under the command of Captain C.Hartley A.V.C. accompanied the Division, the Divisional Hospital remaining at Luton	
18th "	" "	An inspection of all the horses in the Division was made and lists of horses proposed for casting for various reasons were submitted to the G.O.C.	
19th "	" "	A communication was received from Major Johnson A.V.C. in charge of the Notts & Derby Infantry Brigade at Braintree to the effect that an outbreak of Gangrenous Pneumonia had occurred amongst the horses of the Brigade. An inspection was immediately made and a number of horses affected with this disease was found. Five of these animals died and three were sent to the Veterinary Hospital, Stockwood Park. Necessary precautions were taken and no other case has occurred. Over exertion and exposure to inclement weather after arriving at Braintree were undoubtedly the cause of this outbreak.	
21st "	" "	An outbreak of ringworm, chiefly amongst the horses of the Yorkshire Hussars occurred in the Division. Fortunately this was of a mild type and by taking stringent and prompt precautions the outbreak has been checked and is now nearly stamped out.	
25th "	" "	Complaints have been received from Officers Commanding units in the Division of Remounts reissued from Luton. These horses are issued from Remount Depot, Farley Farm, Luton, and not from the Veterinary Hospital at Stockwood Park. It is undoubtedly desirable that an improved system of issuing remounts should be adopted. Horses have been issued quite irrespective of the particular type of animal required. It would be an advantage if Officers commanding units requiring horses informed the O. C. Remount Depot at Farley Farm, Luton, of the number and types of horses required and then each horse issued from Farley Farm be labelled with the name of the unit to which he is issued and the work he is supposed to do.	
31st "	"	Visited the Veterinary Hospital at Luton which has been transferred from Stockwood Park, to the new buildings on the opposite side of the road. I wish to point out that inadequate arrangements have been made at the new hospital. At the present time there are 450 horses in the Hospital and there is only room under the new sheds when completely full, for 250 horses. The sheds in Stockwood Park are still being used and accomodate nearly 100 horses. This leaves another 100 which have to be picketed out, and it would be a great advantage if further sheds were erected to accomodate these horses. I should like to point out that since the Division left Luton, Major Coe, A.V.C. the O.C.the Veterinary Hospital Luton has had to work under great disadvantages. For a long time he was the only Veterinary Officer at the hospital and owing to the removal of the Division a marked increase in the number of horses took place. The Mobile Section marching with the Division took away his only Veterinary Officer and a number of his best N.C.O's and men. At this time a W.O. letter was received decreasing the wages of the civilian horsekeepers	

(1) Veterinary Department

(2) ---------------------

(3) North Midland Division

(4) Stoke on Trent for Veterinary Section.

(5) Derby

(6) Luton, Hertford, Bishops Stortford.

(a) Mobilization took place chiefly at Derby, but several civilian Veterinary Surgeons joined at Luton.

(b) Nil.

(c) Nil.

(d) The training of the personnel of the A.V.C. is chiefly technical. Practical experience is being gained daily.

(e) Discipline is very good.

(f) 1. Nil

2. As horsekeepers willing to serve abroad and to be enlisted are now to be employed at the Veterinary Hospital the difficulty of the civilian element has now been removed.

3. Satisfactory.

4. A suitable cart for the 2nd Mobile Section has yet to be obtained

5. The equipment of the Section is complete with the exception of arms and bandoliers

6. The sheds for the horses at London Road Luton, are now in use but more sheds are required to accomodate the whole of the horses. The huts for the men are at the present time not completely furnished.

7. Correspondence in some matters is very heavy

8. Nil

9. The establishment in remounts is complete. For the most part however they are too small for the purpose required.

(H) Two Veterinary Mobile Sections have already been prepared for Imperial Service

(G) All Officers except four and all the N.C.O's and men have volunteered for service abroad

Bishops Stortford
9/12/14

McDougall
Lt Colonel

Cont'd

31st Nov Bishops Stfd. As a result these left in a body leaving Major Coe with a greatly increased number of horses, no veterinary help and a totally inadequate staff. Under the circumstances it is greatly to his credit that he has been able to carry on. *as efficiently as has been the case.*

Copy

War Diary
(December 1914)

Lt-Colonel MacMDougall
A.D.t.S.
N. Md. Division

Copy

War Diary
(December 1914)

Lt. Colonel W. A. McDougall
A.D.t.S.
A. Md. Director

<u>Copy</u>

Statement for War Diary December 1914.

1) Army Veterinary Services (T.F.)

2) —

3) North Midland Division

4) Stoke on Trent for Divisional Veterinary Hospital.

5) Derby.

6) Luton, Hertford, Bishops Stortford.

(a) Mobilization took place chiefly at Derby but several Civilian Veterinary Surgeons who subsequently were granted commissions, joined at Luton.

(b) —

(c) —

(d) The training of the personnel of the A.V.C. is chiefly technical. Practice experience is being gained daily.

(e) Very good.

(f) 1. Nil
2. The civilian element having ceased to exist the whole question of the personnel is now on a much more satisfactory footing.
3. Satisfactory
4. The N. Mid. Mobile Veterinary Section is now suitably equipped with limbered waggon.
5. The Central Force has intimated that no arms are at present available for the Mobile Vety Section.
6. All the horses under treatment in the Divisional Veterinary Hospital are now under cover viz:- Huts, Stables, Cattle Sheds (Stockwood Park), Farm buildings at Farley Farm.
7.
8.
9. Two Mobile Vety Sections have been already formed but according to the new Establishments require twelve more privates each.
14. When the personnel referred to in 9. is completed and arms issued the N. Mid Mobile Vety Section is prepared.

SKELETON FORM OF WAR DIARY.

      Unit ....

      Brigade ....

      Division...

      Mobilization Centre ....

      Temporary War Station ....

      Stations since occupied subsequent to Concentration :-,

      ....

      ....

(a)   MOBOLIZATION.

(b)   CONCENTRATION AT WAR STATIONS (including Railway Moves)

(c)   ORGANIZATION FOR DEFENCE (including vulnerable points)

(d)   TRAINING.

(e)   DISCIPLINE.

(f)   ADMINISTRATION.

          1.   Medical Services.
          2.   Veterinary Services.
          3.   Supply Services.
          4.   Transport Services.
          5.   Ordnance Services.
          6.   Billeting and Hutting.
          7.   Channels of correspondence in routine matters.
          8.   Range construction.
          9.   Supply of remounts.

(g)   REORGANIZATION OF T. F. INTO HOME AND IMPERIAL SERVICE.

(h)   PREPARATION OF UNITS FOR IMPERIAL SERVICE.

War Diary (December 1914) Lt. Colonel MacDougall
A.D. V.S. N. Mid. Divn.

Date	Place	Information	Remarks

Bishops Stortford — Mange has appeared in several units of the Division and in nearly every case the diagnosis has been confirmed on microscopic examination of scrapings from the skin of the affected horses. The microscopic examination was made by the Veterinary Officers in charge where they were able to obtain the use of a microscope: in cases where this was not possible the scrapings were sent to the Remount Veterinary Hospital Woolwich for examination. All the cases which have occurred up to the present are of the Psoroptic form & the disease has probably been contracted by the farm buildings in which the horses are stabled. Mange I understand was prevalent in certain farms and in so far as I have been able to learn the farm owners by the horses of the Division were not affected but there are I think easy to learn the two facts in connection with the matter. If anything the heavy & pretty coats of the horses when they were housed under cover in farm buildings predisposed them to become affected with mange as will be shown by the sequel. All the affected horses has been sent to the Div. Vety Hospital for treatment with the exception of the cases at Saffron Walden (3rd Field Ambulance A.S.C. + Staff, Infantry Brigade) where it was possible to make satisfactory arrangements in dealing with them. Locally Lieut R. J. Price A.V.C.(T.F.) is dealing with the outbreak at Saffron Walden and appears to be getting it well in hand. The form of mange now existing in the Division viz. Psoroptic Mange is much more easily cured than the other form, Sarcoptic Mange. Owing to the parasite (acarus) living on the surface of the skin & being easily got at with suitable dressings after the horse has been clipped. The Sarcoptic on the other hand is more difficult to deal with.

Strangles. The epizootic is practically over. The majority of the horses are returning to their work in good condition. The cases of this disease which are now occurring are in the new Ammunition Columns the horses of these & other units being now "salted" or immune.

Veterinary Arrangements. A complaint was made to me on 9th Jany 1915 that no veterinary arrangements had been made for the horses of the 1st Field Coy R.E. (1st Reserve). The complaint was the first intimation that I had that this unit existed. I think when new units are formed or when units are moved that the A.D.V.S. of the Division should be told from some reliable official source of these events & that he should not be left to find out by accident or chance days or perhaps weeks afterwards.

Veterinary Officers. The supply of Veterinary Officers for the Territorial Force appears to be inadequate. The Regular Army is taking every available man. The Division is three Veterinary Officers short. Every effort has been made to fill these vacancies but it has not been possible to do so up to the present.

MacDougall
Lt Colonel
Bishops Stortford   A.D.V.S. North Midland Division
10th Jany 1915

Copy

Statement for War Diary December 1914.

1) Army Veterinary Services (T.F.)
2) —
3) North Midland Division.
4) Stoke on Trent for Divisional Veterinary Hospital.
5) Derby.
6) Luton, Hertford, Bishops Stortford.

(a) Mobilization took place chiefly at Derby but several Civilian Veterinary Surgeons who subsequently were granted commissions, joined at Luton.

(b) — — — — — —
(c) — — — — — —

(d) The training of the personnel of the A.V.C. is chiefly technical. Practice experience is being gained daily.

(e) Very good.

(f) 1. Nil
2. The civilian element having ceased to exist the whole question of the personnel is now on a much more satisfactory footing.
3. Satisfactory
4. The N. Mid. Mobile Veterinary Section is now suitably equipped with limbered waggon.
5. The Central Force has intimated that no arms are at present available for the Mobile Vety Section.
6. All the horses under treatment in the Divisional Veterinary Hospital are now under cover viz:- Huts, Stables, Cattle Sheds (Clockwood Park), Farm buildings at Farley Farm.
7. —
8. —

g. 9. Two Mobile Vety Sections have been already formed but according to the new Establishments require twelve more privates each.

h. When the personnel referred to in g is completed and arms issued the N. Mid Mobile Vety Section is prepared.

SKELETON FORM OF WAR DIARY.

Unit ....

Brigade ....

Division ....

Mobilization Centre ....

Temporary War Station ....

Stations since occupied subsequent to Concentration :-,

....

....

(a) MOBOLIZATION.
(b) CONCENTRATION AT WAR STATIONS (including Railway Moves)
(c) ORGANIZATION FOR DEFENCE (including vulnerable points)
(d) TRAINING.
(e) DISCIPLINE.
(f) ADMINISTRATION.
    1. Medical Services.
    2. Veterinary Services.
    3. Supply Services.
    4. Transport Services.
    5. Ordnance Services.
    6. Billeting and Hutting.
    7. Channels of correspondence in routine matters.
    8. Range construction.
    9. Supply of remounts.
(g) REORGANIZATION OF T. F. INTO HOME AND IMPERIAL SERVICE.
(h) PREPARATION OF UNITS FOR IMPERIAL SERVICE.

Subject :- War Diaries.   C O N F I D E N T I A L .   N.M D.
                                   999------------------   142/G.

Headquarters,
    A.D.V.S.

1. There has been considerable trouble in connection with the November War Diaries.
2. The careful attention of all concerned is directed to :-
    (i) This office above number of 15th September.
    (ii) This office above number of 22nd September, forwarding a circular memorandum from Central Force.
    (iii) IIIrd Army Order No. 108 of 14th October 1914.
3. The chief object of the Diary in the present instance is "to record information for future reference" (F.S.R. Pt.II, Sec: 140 para 1 (ii))
    There is however no objection to entering the nature of the training done each day, as this record is very decidedly useful for future reference; but schemes of operations will not be attached as Appendices to the copy forwarded to Divisional Headquarters. No such entry as "Church Parade" for instance should find a place in the Diary.
4. In addition to the diary, there will be forwarded in duplicate with each diary, a "STATEMENT" (see attached form) dealing with the lessons gained from experience during the month.
5. Officers Commanding Formations will comment as necessary on the "STATEMENTS" of each Unit, saying whether they agree with the conclusions reached, or not, and if not why not.
    In the "STATEMENTS" attached to their own diaries by Officers Commanding Formations, the latter will not only make their own remarks as advisable, but will also summarise the conclusions reached by Officers Commanding Units and shown in each Unit's "STATEMENT".
6. In this way it should only be necessary for Divisional Officers to study the STATEMENTS and diaries of the Officers Commanding Formations; similarly it should only be necessary for Army Corps Officers to study those of Divisions.
7. This work requires very real care and attention, which in the end saves labour to everyone. The utmost conciseness must be aimed at in these STATEMENTS and no encouragement given to the tendency shown by some officers to use this opportunity for a monthly grumble.
8. Diaries and STATEMENTS are required to reach this office on the 10th of each month at the latest. They will not be forwarded one by one, but will be collected by Officers Commanding Formations and forwarded with the Formation STATEMENT in one batch.

Bishop's Stortford.

29th December 1914.

                                                    WWWeber
                                                    Lieut-Colonel,
                                    General Staff, North Midland Division T.F.

The headings under which the "STATEMENT" is required are :-

(a) Mobilization.

(b) Concentration at War Stations.

(c) Vulnerable Points.

(d) Training.

(e) Discipline.

(f) Administration :-

    1. Medical Services.
    2. Veterinary Services.
    3. Supply Services.
    4. Transport Services.
    5. Ordnance Services.
    6. Billeting & Hutting.
    7. Channels of correspondence in Routine Matters.
    8. Remounts.

(g) Re-organization into Home and Imperial Service Units.

(h) Preparation for Imperial Service.

(i) Miscellaneous.

This list is a guide only. It is absolutely unnecessary to report under each heading because that heading is mentioned.

Colonel G.F.R.Henderson said of such a list of headings -

"Make a slave of it not a master". Remarks should usually be confined to cases where the writer has a point to make which will affect the future. A definite recommendation should generally accompany a tale of trouble.

                                                W.F.W.

Office Copy

STATEMENT FOR WAR DIARY, JANUARY, 1915.

1. Army Veterinary Services.
2. ------------------
3. North Midland Division.
4. Stoke on Trent for Divisional Veterinary Hospital.
5. Derby.
6. Luton, Hertford, Bishops Stortford.

   (a) Mobilization took place chiefly at Derby, but the personnel was completed at Luton.

   (b) ----------

   (c) ,,----------

   (d) The training of the personnel of the A.V.C. is chiefly technical. Practical experience is being gained daily.

   (e) Very Good

   (f) 1. Nil

      2. The civilian element having ceased to exsist the personnel is now on a much more satisfactory footing.

      3. Satisfactory.

      4. Satisfactory

      5. ----------------

      6. Satisfactory.

      7. ----------------

      8. ----------------

      9. ----------------

   (g) The two Mobile veterinary Sections raised by the North Midland Division, have been increased by twelve Privates each, in accordance with the latest Establishment.

   (h) The North Midland Mobile Veterinary Section is prepared, except in so far as it has had no arms issued to it, or any training in the use of arms.

Bishops Stortford
8th Feby 1915

A. McDougall
Lt-Colonel
A.D.V.S. N. Md. Division

Copy

Summary of Information

WAR DIARY (JANUARY 1915) Lt Colonel W.A.McDougall.A.D.V.S.N.Mid.Divn.

Date.	Place.		Remarks
January.	Bishops Stortford.		Mange still exsists in several units of the Division and fresh cases have occurred during the month, but the increase in the number of cases has not been great and leads one to hope that the steps taken to prevent the spread of the disease are having the desired effect. Regular veterinary inspections of all horse's skins are made at short intervals by the veterinary officers in charge and anything of a suspicious nature is brought to the notice of the A.D.V.S. In accordance with Central Force order No 66, dated 19th January, horses suffering from contagious skin diseases are not now sent to the Divisional Veterinary Hospital but the veterinary officer in charge of each brigade arranges for the segregation and treatment of those cases, a small isolation hospital being formed for the brigade when necessary. Many of the cases of mange which were under treatment last month are now apparently cured, and are being put to work under a system of working isolation. A large number of horses are effected with Lice. This is largely a question depending on the kind of stable management which exsists and some units are more affected than others. RINGWORM. There has been a considerable decrease in the number of cases of this disease reported during the month. Strangles and catarrh are practically non-existent in the units of the Division except in the Divisional Ammunition Column. The horses of the last named unit are new, fresh, horses, and are going sick in large numbers from those diseases. A serious outbreak of contagious pneumonia has also occurred in this unit. Army Forms 0.1640. There has been considerable difficulty in getting units to pass those forms when horses are transferred to the Divisional Veterinary Hospital and also difficulty in getting them to sign the receipt portion when horses have been returned from the Divisional Veterinary Hospital to the Units. The trouble in connection with those forms is, however, I think less than it was some weeks ago. Corn crushers, and chaff cutters. In spite of repeated efforts on the part of the O.C.Divisional Veterinary Hospital and myself no corn crushers or chaff cutters have yet been issued to the Veterinary Hospital. The Ordnance Department have been repeatedly asked to supply those articles but without any result up to the present. VETERINARY OFFICERS. Two more veterinary officers are required to complete the establishment of the Division but I have been unable up to the present to obtain any.

WMcDougall Lt Colonel. A.D.V.S.N.Mid.Divn

No War Diary for
February.

Division left BISHOPS STORTFORD for France on 26th Feb 1915

121/6390

46th Division

A.D.V.S. 46th Division

Vol I

1-3-31-4-15

<u>Confidential</u>

War Diary
of
Lt-Colonel Maur. Dougall
A.D.V.S. 46th (North Midland) Division
T.F.

From 1st March 1915   To 31st July 1915.

(Volume I)

46th Division

12/6390

A.D.V.S. 46th Division

Vol I

1-3-15 - 31-4-15

Confidential

War Diary
of
Lt. Colonel Wm. MacDougall
A.D.V.S. 46th (North Midland) Division
T.F.

From 1st March 1915   To 31st July 1915.

(Volume I)

War Diary of Lt. Colonel J.A. McDougall A.D.V.S. 46th (North Midland) Division from 1st March to 31st July 1915.

Date	Place	
		I disembarked at Le Havre on 28th February 1915 with the Headquarters of the 1st North Midland Division T.F. (now 46th (N. Mid) Division) and have been serving with that Division as A.D.V.S. ever since. A War Diary was handed in by me each month from date of Mobilization up to the time of leaving England but since arrival in this country I have not been called on to furnish a Diary until now. According to Field Service Regns. Part II I see that a War Diary should have been rendered on the last day of each month to the officer i/c the A.G.'s Office of the Base & it is regretted that by an oversight this has not been done. In future this will be done each month. The Diary which I now forward covers the period 1st March to 31st July.
1st March — 31st July 1915		**Injured necks.** An embarkation order was in existence at the time this Division embarked for abroad to the effect that the horses nosebags were to be suspended round the horses necks prior to their being embarked. These nosebags as a rule contained about 12 lbs of Corn. A large number of horses sustained serious injury to their necks as a result of these nose bags being carried round the neck. This was especially so in hogged horses. A few hours suspension of the heavy bag was sufficient to cause injury, & the injuries caused in this way ranged from a slight abrasion to an injury of the most serious kind necessitating months of treatment & probably in some cases destruction. The worst of these cases were of course evacuated to Veterinary Hospitals on the L of C. Attention was called to this matter by me to the proper authorities at this time. The horses stood the voyage &c. well, & barring the injured necks referred to, suffered little.
		Cracked Heels. Heavy draught horses especially suffered particularly during the wet muddy weather when we first came out from sloughy wounds about the pasterns & coronets. This condition became much less frequent when the weather & the ground dried up, but it has never entirely disappeared. Cases continuing to occur amongst heavy horses to a limited extent.
		Mares in foal. A considerable number of in foal mares were evacuated during the period middle of April to middle of June. All in foal mares were evacuated & four mares foaled while still with the Division, & were evacuated later with foal at foot.
		Mange. Has not existed to any extent in the Division, but since the month of June a few odd cases have occurred. During the last month the Units have had cases (a limited number), these were immediately dealt with & the spread of the disease appears to have been checked.
		General Condition & Management of horses. The general condition of the horses is good, & the horsemastership & general management is also good. The improvement in horsemastership since the Division was mobilized has been very great indeed.
		Shoeing. The shoeing on the whole is good, & the Farriers & Shoeing Smiths are in most instances capable workmen. Difficulty has been experienced at times in altering & fitting shoes especially of heavy horses & the lighter horses which require special shoeing. These difficulties do not exist where the use of a Divisional Forge can be obtained, but where the use of such a forge is not available, & when no Field Forge & Anvil are on charge, the shoes, especially heavy ones, cannot be altered & the horses feet suffer in consequence.
July		**Forage.** The forage supplied to the Division has on the whole been very good. More hay would have been advantageous but since a certain amount of green stuff & grazing has been available, the horses have done well. The actual sickness is now & has been for sometime very small, the chief casualties being lameness, injuries, kicks, wounds &c. **Personnel.** The A.V.C. personnel officers N.C.O's & men is practically up to strength & is efficient.

J.A. McDougall
Lt. Colonel
A.D.V.S. 46th (North Midland) Division T.F.

46th Division

Confidential.

War Diary of
Lt-Colonel MacDougall.
A.D.V.S. 46th (North Midland) Division
T.F.

121/6753

From   To ✓
1st August 1915.   31st August 1915.

Pt II

N   ✓

46th Division

Confidential.

War Diary of
Lt. Colonel MacDougall.
A.D.V.S. 46th (North Midland) Division
T.F.

$\frac{121}{6753}$

From
1st August 1915

To
31st August 1915.

Vol II

War Diary of Lt-Colonel W.A.M.Dougall, A.D.V.S. 46th (North Midland) Division
for month of August 1915.

Date	Place	
1915 8th Augst		Lieut. H.C. Taylor A.V.C. (T.F.) admitted to Hospital
9th "		Lieut. J.L. Crane A.V.C. (T.F.) admitted to Hospital
10th "		" " " " " " evacuated from Divisional Rest Station to a Base Hospital
12th & 18th		Lt Colonel W.A.M.Dougall on Short leave to England (first leave since arrival in the country)
17th Augst		Lieut. H.C. Taylor A.V.C. (T.F.) evacuated to England
18th "		" " " " " " " " " went before a Medical Board in London & was granted three weeks leave. I received a letter from Lieut Taylor from his home at Caistor, Lincolnshire, informing me of this.
21st August to 2nd Sept		Leave to England was granted to Captain W.T. Sadler A.V.C. (T.F.) from 21st August to 4th September, on urgent business affairs. Capt Sadler rejoined the Division on the morning of Friday 3rd Sept. and resumed duty from that date.
17th Augst		The Veterinary duties connected with the 5th Corps Headquarters were taken over by the 46th (N.Mid.) Division from the 4th Division under orders received from the 2nd Army (D.D.V.S.). Capt C. Hartley A.V.C (T.F.) being put ic/ of the 5th Corps H.Q. lines, Cable Section R.E. & the Combat. Forties Coy R.E. and Lieut W.G. Thomson A.V.C (T.F.) i/c S.C. & L.J.Co Section R.E.
		Several outbreaks of Foot & Mouth disease have been diagnosed by Officers A.V.C of the Division, & myself during the month amongst Cattle belonging to Belgian & French farmers & action taken in accordance with the late B.E.F Hors. Circular Memo. on this subject.
28th Augst		Lieut. J Facer A.V.C (T.F.) sick in his tent where he remained until removed to the Divisional Rest Station on 3rd Sept. 1915.
28th "		Lieut. W.G. Thomson A.V.C (T.F.) granted short leave to England from 28/8/15 to 3/9/15.

W.A.M.Dougall
Lt Colonel
A.D.V.S. 46th (North Midland) Division. T.F.

7th Sept. 1915.

121/7145.

46th Division

A.D.V.S. 48th Division

Vol III

Sept 15.

Confidential

War Diary of
Lt. Colonel MacDougall
A.D.␣.S. 46th (N.Mid) Division.
T.F.

From
1st Septr 1915

To
30th Septr 1915

121/7145.

46th Division

A.D.V.S. 46th Division

Vol III

Sept 15.

Confidential

War Diary of
Lt. Colonel MacDougall.
A.D.t.S. 46th (N.Mid) Division.
T.F.

From
1st Sept. 1915.

To
30th Sept. 1915.

War Diary of Lt-Colonel MacDougall A.D.V.S. 46th (N.Mid) Division
for month of September 1915

Date	Place	Remarks
1915		
3 Sept		Lieut. J. Facer A.V.C.(T.F.) admitted to Hospital.
"		A special report from each V.O. was called for on the subject of picked up nails with special reference to the "travelling field cooker" as a distributor. The consensus of opinion was that the "travelling field cooker" did not play an important part in the distribution of nails & with certain patterns of cookers, there was no chance of nails being distributed.
"		Lieut. H. Newton A.V.C.(T.F.) admitted to Hospital.
"		Lance-Corporal J. Simpson A.V.C.(T.F.) attached to 137th Infantry Brigade promoted to the rank of Temporary Sergeant. Authority D.V.S. 2/4231/15 dated 10/9/15.
"		Lieut. H. Newton returned to duty from Hospital.
"		Lieut. J. Facer " " " "
"		Captain F. Douthwaite proceed on 7 days leave to the U.K. Period of leave to date 19th to 25th Sept. inclusive.
(NM2)		Sergeant Wm. Hagarth A.V.C.(T.F.) transferred to 138th Infantry Bgde from 46th N.Mid Mobile Veterinary Section.
(NM4)		Corporal W. Graham A.V.C.(T.F.) promoted to Temporary Sergeant & transferred from 46th N.Mid M.V.S. to 139th Infantry Brigade.
"		Lance-Corporals J. Hollis and B. Brain A.V.C.(T.F.) transferred from 137th and 138th Infantry Bgdes respectively, to 46th N.Mid. M.V.S. and reverted to their substantive rank of Private.
30		Recommendations for "consistent good service rendered in such a manner as to merit reward" for months of April to August 1915 inclusive, for officers, N.C.O.s & men A.V.C.(T.F.) 46th Division rendered to Div. Headquarters & to A.D.V.S. 2nd Army.
"		One additional officer recommended on 26/9/15.

M.MacDougall
Lt Colonel
A.D.V.S. 46th (N.Mid) Division.

30th Sept. 1915

46th Division

121/7381

Confidential

War Diary
of
Lt. Colonel W.A. McDougall.
A.D.v.S. 46th (North Midland)
Division.

From
1st October 1915

To
31st October 1915.

Vol IV

46th Division

121/7381

Confidential

War Diary
of
Lt. Colonel W. MacDougall.
A.D.V.S. 46th (North Midland)
Division.

From
1st October 1915

To
31st October 1915.

Vol IV

War Diary of Lt-Colonel W.A.M. Dougall A.D.V.S. 46th (North Midland) Division

Date	Place	Remarks
Oct 3rd		Division moved from 2nd Army to 1st Army. I rode from one area to the other & arrived at Gonnay on 6th Oct: 1915.
" 7th		Lieut N.C. Taylor A.V.C.(T.F.) rejoined the Division from the United Kingdom to which country he had been evacuated sick on 17th August 1915.
" 9th		D.D.V.S. 1st Army inspected the 46th held M.V.S. and saw some of the V.Os of the Division.
" 12th		Received orders to the effect that Captain M.T. Sadler A.V.C.(T.F.) was to proceed to England without delay and report himself to A.D.V.S. 2/1st North Midland Division at St Albans.
" 13th		Captain M.T. Sadler reported his departure en route to St Albans.
" 17th		Orders received from D.D.V.S. 1st Army through XI Corps that one Officer A.V.C.(T.F.) was to be transferred without delay from 46th Division to 1st Division.
" 18th		Lieut. F.J. Redmond A.V.C.(T.F.) proceeded to join 1st Division.
" 24th		Division moved from Gonnay to a new area i.e. to Fouquires-les-Bethune.
" 28th		Received Orders from D.D.V.S. 1st Army through XI Corps that one Officer A.V.C.(T.F.) was to proceed from 46th Division to 50th (Northumbrian) Division for duty.
" 29th		Lieut. C.H. Newton A.V.C.(T.F.) proceeded to join the 50th (Northumbrian) Division.
" 30th		Lieut. C.R. Evans A.V.C.(T.F.) rejoined the Division from England where he had been on leave & had been twice granted an extension of leave on account of sickness.
		Attended a Conference of A.D.V.Ss of 1st Army at Locon.

W.A.M. Dougall
Lt. Colonel
A.D.V.S. 46th (North Midland)
Division

Confidential

War Diary
of
Lt. Colonel MacDougall
A.D.V.S. 46th (N.Md.) Division

From
1st November 1915

To
30th November 1915.

(Volume 5) V

Confidential

War Diary

of

Lt. Colonel MacDougall
A.D.V.S. 46th (N. Mid.) Division

From
1st November 1915

To
30th November 1915

(Volume) V

War Diary of Lt-Colonel M. McDugall A.D.V.S. 46th (North Midland) Division

Date 1915	Place	Remarks of A.D.V.S.
1st Novr		Lieut. J. L. Crane A.V.C. (T.F.) ordered to join Indian Veterinary Hospital, Rouen. This Officer rejoined the 46th Division on 30/10/15 from sick leave in England.
2nd "		Lieut. J. L. Crane reported his departure to join Indian Vety. Hospital, Rouen.
4th "		46th N. Mid. M.V.S. moved from Vergies to La Fosse.
4th "		A.D.V.S.'s Office moved from Fouquieres (Bethune) to La Fosse.
5th "	La Fosse	Capt. G. F. Budge A.V.C. (Temporary Commission) V.O. i/c 2nd Heavy Brigade R.G.A. N.A.R. billeted in N. Midd. Divisional Area reported himself to A.D.V.S.
6th "		Visit of A.D.V.S. 1st Army (Lt Colonel Newsom)
7th "		Visit of A.D.V.S. 1st Army & Lt. Colonel E.E. Martin the latter officer having just taken up the appointment of A.D.V.S. 1st Army.
7th "		46th N. Mid. M.V.S. moved from La Fosse to Rue de ? (Bethune Combined Sdg).
8th "		Two cases of Sarcoptic Mange were diagnosed in the 26th London Battery 2nd Hy Bde R.G.A. N.A.R. temporarily attached to 46th Div. for administrative purposes. The horses were evacuated.
13th "		Two cases of Sarcoptic Mange were diagnosed amongst Divl. R. of Horses (viz. the two Chargers of Lt Colonel Game C.R.E.) The horses were evacuated. The number of cases of "picked up nails" have greatly increased during the month of Novr. Also cases of "necrotic sloughs". The latter are accounted for I think by the fact that the weather was wet & cold, & the horses were standing perpetually in deep mud. Brick standings &c. not having been made. The Division which the 46th Divn. took over from having apparently done very little in the way of making standings for horses. Kicks have decreased considerably which is accounted for largely by the fact that heel-ropes are now used much more extensively than was the case previously. Great progress was made by all the Units of the Division in the way of making standings for horses but only in a few instances were they ready to put horses on by the end of the month. The 46th Division has been I think particularly unfortunate regarding standings for horses all units have worked in making standings & on at least four occasions these standings have been either completed or nearly so when the Division was moved to a new area; And in hardly any of these new areas did they go into billets where standings existed.

M. McDugall
Lt Colonel
A.D.V.S. 46th N. Mid. Division

46th/5W

Confidential

War Diary
of
Lt-Colonel W.A. McDougall
A.D.V.S. 46th (N. Mid^d)
Division.

From
1st Decr 1915.

To
31st Decr 1915.

(Volume 6)

46th/5w

<u>Confidential</u>

War Diary
of
Lt-Colonel W.A.M. Dougall
A.D.V.S. 46th (N. Mid.)
Division.

From
1st Decr 1915.

To
31st Decr 1915.

(Volume 6)

War Diary of Lt-Colonel W.A. McDougall A.D.V.S. 46th North Midland Division.

Date	Place	Remarks
1915		
5th Decr		The Division moved from Lestrem & vicinity to St Venant, and began preparing for move to another country.
7th "		All Heavy Draught horses of the Division are being exchanged for Light Draughts and Mules, and this began in the case of some Units on this date. Animals were exchanged with the 2nd, Guards, 19th Divisions & G.H.Q. The Heavy Draught horses of the 46th Divr. were a particularly good lot, and on the whole the Division did not have the best of the exchange. In some cases the exchanges were satisfactory, this Division, but in others they were not. A large number of animals received were evacuated to Base Veterinary Hospitals within a few days of being received for Debility, Lameness and other causes. In the case of one Unit the percentage of evacuations was as high as 40 per cent. And in a few other cases the animals received were returned to the Units from which they came. This was the case in the 1st Ammunition Column 1st N. Midd. Brigade R.F.A. 54 Mules being returned to the 33rd D.A.C. The exchanges were carried out in a great hurry which no doubt accounted for the arrangements being unsatisfactory so far as certain Units were concerned, but when it is left to Units to send any animals they like they are not likely to send their best and in many instances they sent their worst. Mallein testing. The Mallein testing of all animals of this Divn. began on 7/12/15 - Intra-dermal palpebral Method. This testing was carried out under very adverse conditions as the weather was bad, the country wet and low lying, and the animals were in most instances standing up to their knees and hocks in mud, but notwithstanding all these disadvantages the testing of all animals was satisfactorily carried out by the Veterinary Officers. Two horses both Officers chargers of 2nd N. Midd. Bde. R.F.A. reacted, & reacted when re-tested a second time. They were both destroyed but no Glander's lesions were found on post-mortem. The Mallein testing took nearly a fortnight.
10th Decr		G.O.C. 46th Division inspected the men of the 46th N. Midd. Mobile Veterinary Section. Only the men were inspected - A dismounted Parade.
15th Decr		A Redistribution of the duties of the Officers A.V.C. (T.F.) was made on this date, in view of the Division proceeding overseas.
19th "		Divl. Headquarters moved to Lambres. Sergeant J Simpson A.V.C. (T.F.) attached to 137th Infantry Brigade was put under arrest for drunkenness on line of march and was afterwards awarded 28 days F.P. No 1 by Brigade Commander, & reduced to his substantive rank of Private.
25th "		Corporal H Dawson A.V.C. (T.F.) was attached to 137th Infantry Brigade from M.V.S. and given the Temporary rank of Sergeant, to take over duties previously performed by Sergeant Simpson.
28th "		The Mallein testing of all the horses of 2nd N. Midd. Bde. R.F.A. was begun on 25th and completed on 28/12/15. No reactors. A large number of horses & mules with necrotic sloughs have been evacuated during the month due to constantly standing in mud. Although Units have repeatedly made standings they have usually moved before they were ready to be used and in very few instances were they fortunate enough to find standings ready made in the new area.

W.A. McDougall
Lt Colnl.
A.D.V.S. 46th (N. Midd.) Division.

A.D.V.S. 46th Divn.

Sam

Vol VII

Confidential

War Diary of
Lt-Colonel M.A.McDougall
A.D.V.S. 46th (North Midland)
Division. T.F.

From   To
1st January 1916.   31st January 1916.

(Volume 7)

A.D.V.S. 46th Division

Sam

vol VII

Confidential

War Diary of
Lt-Colonel M.A. MacDougall
A.D.V.S. 46th (North Midland)
Division. T.F.

From
1st January 1916

To
31st January 1916.

(Volume 4)

War Diary of Lt-Colonel W. McDougall. A.D.V.S. 46th (North Midland) Division.

Date	Place	Remarks
1916 7th January		Received a report from Headquarters 139th Infantry Brigade that No 4/4 Sergeant W Graham A.V.C.(T.F.) attached to 139th Infy Bgde had been missing since 2nd January 1916 and that he was supposed to have been drowned in the Canal near Isbergues. A search was made for him & the canal dragged at the place where he was thought to have got into the canal, & where a horse was seen scrambling out of the Canal on 2/1/16. Sergeant Graham's horse was caught on the Road near Berguette Lock closing on night of 2/1/16 & showed evidence of having been in the water. It is not known how this N.C.O. got into the canal & no one appears to have seen him in the water. The mare he was riding had a bad character & had run away with several people before he got her. Some of the Infantry of the Division have already entrained en route for some place overseas but as far as no animals have been entrained.
6th to 14th Jany		All the animals of the Division except those of 3rd N Mid Bde R.F.A. and 1/1st and 1/3rd Field Coys R.E. and 1/1st N Mid Mobile Vety Section where entrained at Berguette & Lillers en route for Marseilles & Overseas. The Divisional train & So A.C. not accompanying the Division.
17th Jany		Proceeded to Marseilles by ordinary train as my services were required there & I had been wired for. No animals were left about the country up to the time of my departure everything having been collected & disposed of. Captain C Hartley Commanding M.V.S. was left behind in charge of all Veterinary matters. & one V.O. (Lieut J A Shaw A.V.C.(T.F.)) was with 3rd N Mid Bde R.F.A.
4 to 7th Jany		I arrived at Marseilles on morning of 19/1/16 & found that about 500 animals had already been embarked & had sailed, the remainder being in Camp at Valentine & Borely Camps. Captain F Douthwaite A.V.C (T.F) acted as S.V.O. 46th Division at Marseilles & was sent on with the first lot of horses with that object in view & so that he could make all necessary veterinary arrangements until I arrived there. The animals which had proceed overseas were the transport of the 137th Infantry Brigade & the 1st Monmouth Regt. Sergeant N Dawson A.V.C.(T.F.) proceeded with the 137th Infty Bgde but not all Sick & Lame horses at Marseilles were sent to Indian Vety Hospital Le Valentine Camp, & animals to replace them were issued from Indian Remount Depot at the same place. As the embarking of the remainder of the Division was stopped & the Units in Marseilles sent back up country by train. I remained in Marseilles until practically all animals had been entrained & then proceeded up country. No horse died on the journey north & certain minor casualties occurred but on the whole nothing serious occurred - rubbed tails & big galls were the chief injuries. The Division joined the 3rd Army on arrival up country but the Units which proceeded overseas have not yet joined up with the rest of the Division. The Units - including 1/1st N Mid M.V.S. - which had not proceeded overseas or to Marseilles has joined 3rd Army from 1st Army area by the time I arrived.
29th Jany		I arrived at Divisional Headquarters in 3rd Army area from Marseilles on 29/1/16.

W.McDougall.
Lt-Colonel
A.D.V.S. 46th Division.

Confidential.

War Diary of
Lt. Colonel MacDougall
A.D.V.S. 46th (North Midland)
Division T.F.

From
1st Feby 1916

To
29th February 1916.

(Volume 8)

War Diary of Lt. Colonel M.W. McDougal A.D.M.S. 46th (N. Mid.) Division

Date	Place	Remarks
1916 Feby	Pont Remy	
" 20th		Portion of the Division is and round Pont Remy waiting for the remainder of the Division to return from overseas. Units widely scattered.
		Divisional Headquarters moved from Pont Remy to Rimaucourt. Heavy fall of snow which lasted for about a week with sharp frost making travelling on the roads (with horses very difficult. There was a scarcity of frost dogs & frost nails.
		Lectures on Trench Attacks of mines to officers at 60 classes at 3rd Army Artillery School at Mailleumer.
" 24th		Divisional Headquarters moved to Doullens.
" 29th		I have only been able to get the use of a Motor Car once during the month, fifteen out of the Divisional M.T. Coy Cars as they were urgently needed by the Staff. As the Units of the Division were widely scattered & the distances great, I was not able to carry out many inspections.

M.W. McDougal
Lt. Colonel
A.D.M.S. 46th Division

Confidential

War Diary
of
Lt. Colonel W.A.McDougall
A.D.V.S. 46th (N.Mid.d) Division
T.F.

From
1st March 1916

To
31st March 1916

(Volume 9)

War Diary of Lt Colonel WW Brugel ADC & 16th V Field Howitzers

Date	Place	Remarks
1910 March 3rd		Lectured to Officers and also to NCO's class at 3rd Army Artillery School "HAVERINS"
" 6th		Personal HQrs moved from DOULLENS to LE CAUROY
" 7th		LE CAUROY to CHAMBLAIN L'ABBE
" 14th		D.A. & 3rd Army inspected horses of 1st, 2nd, 3rd, 4th & 5th My & 16th Staffordshire Battery
" 20th		Inspected horses of 3rd F. Med. Regts D.F.A. with Divisional Commander.
		Quarterly report to now submitted by A.D. & S to Brig Genl for inspection of D.O.C.
		A.D. & S attached a conference on Tuesday & Thursday at 6 PM which is presided over by O.D.C. which will deal with everything that is connected with Plumbing etc
" 27th March		Staff Officers inspected of Large Draught Horses from Leicester Regiment. Also 3 Contract Animals.
" 26 "		Proceeded on short tour to England

War Diary of
Lt. Colonel M. an. Dougall
A.D.V.S. 46th (N.Mid.) Division.

From
1st April 1916

To
30th April 1916.

(Volume X (1916))

War Diary of
Lt. Colonel Wand-Dougall.
A.D.M.S. 46th (N.Mid.) Division.

From
1st April 1916

To
30th April 1916.

(Volume X 1916)

War Diary of Lt-Colonel MacDougall A.D.V.S. 46th (N. Mid) Division for April 1916.

	On leave in England until 13th April 1916. (29/3/16 to 13/4/16)
5/4/16	G.O.C. 17th Corps inspected the horses of the 46th Divisional Artillery. Capt. E. Hartley R.VC (T.F.) who was acting as A.D.V.S. during my absence attended inspection. The horses of some of the R.A. Units towards the end of the winter were in poor condition; this is I think to be accounted for by the conditions under which these animals had to live viz. the shortage in the ration of hay (5 lbs of hay being all their ration for a considerable time), & also to lack of Officer Supervision & good horsemastership generally. When the Guns are in action there is practically no Officer Supervision. All the Officers & best N.C.O.s are with the Guns. Occasionally an officer is back with the horses but it often happens that he is young & inexperienced or both. The lack of proper Officer supervision in the Horse Lines of R.A. Units when the Guns are in action tells against the Welfare of the horses.
25/4/16	D.D.V.S. 3rd Army inspected the animals of Nos. 1 & 3 Sections & H.Q. of 46th D.A.C. — No 2 Section being absent on detached duty in the area of another Division.
30/4/16	Received instructions regarding the new scale of Veterinary equipment which has been approved by D.V.S. and steps are being taken to call in the Surplus from Units, and indent for deficiencies so that the new scale may be brought into effect. The withdrawal of the 8 lb tin Zinc Oxide & the substitution of 2.5 lbs Poly Cresto will leave Units without such useful & necessary articles as Enema syringe, Tooth rasps & Brass Dressing syringes. I am putting forward a request to be allowed to retain these articles.

MacDougall
Lt-Colonel
A.D.V.S. 46th (N. Mid) Division.

Army Form C. 2118.

WAR DIARY

INTELLIGENCE SUMMARY of A.D.V.S. 46th (North Midland) Division.

(Erase heading not required.) For May 1916.

Vol XI

Place	Date	Hour	Summary of Events and Information	Remarks and references to Appendices
	3/5/16		A.D.V.S. 3rd Army inspected No. 2 Section B.R.S. at Maricourt St Pol. This Section had just returned from work in connection with a light railway near firing line.	
	5/5/16		File received in the Comdt. Horse of 1/1 S.M.M. Mob. Vety Sect. at Bruay at which this Unit was billetted at Boulevard Divisional 2 am by the Sentry. Two men were sleeping in loft above, they were without being disturbed at all, but one of their kits belonging was written. The Comdt. horse was a much then so forfeiting Guard a Farm buick. The Comdt. horse was entirely dewinded of & Court of Inquiry assembled from proceeding to rest of farm buildings. A Court of Inquiry assembled to investigate the circumstances in accordance with the operating orders.	
	8/5/16		Three units to tow remainder of Divisional H.Q. from St. Michel to P.43.	
	10/5/16		Captain F. Douthwaite proceeded on leave to England for usual term	
	22/5/16		Lt. Colonel W.A.M. Dougall proceeded to 3rd Army H.Q. & to Sect. as D.D.V.S. during absence on leave of Lt. Colonel K.D. Beg. Captain C. Hartley acting as A.D.V.S. 46th (N. Mid) Divin. & Captain J. the Faur A.V.C. (T.F.) acting as D.A.D.V.S. 46 (N. Mid) M.D.	

W.A.M.Dougall
Lt. Colonel
A.D.V.S. 46th (N. Mid) Division.

WAR DIARY / INTELLIGENCE SUMMARY

Army Form C. 2118.

of Lt. Col. Sub (W. McDonagh) A.D.V.S. 46th (N. Mid) Division

June 1916

Vol 12

46

Place	Date	Hour	Summary of Events and Information	Remarks and references to Appendices
Pas	1/6/16		Lt.Col Wainsborough returned from 3rd Army HQrs & resumed his duties of A.D.V.S. 46.	
	2/6/16		Lt.Col R.G. Ace D.D.V.S. 3rd Army inspected the horses of B (South Staff) Battery at 8 P.M. Jor. This division. He decided to evacuate 11 Eighty six of which had been declared by Mauricers under observation. The invalids of the horses, all of which, were apparently healthy, as to the horses. Agreed with Col. Sub decide as a precautionary measure, & turned to hard ground. All the other invalid Mauricers are being taken to the netreat. (Excepts MSS)	
	3/6/16		He asked the netreat. Divisional Commander inspected horses of B (South Staff) Battery & also tests in M.V.S which were to be evacuated the following day.	
	4/6/16		Sunday	
	5/6/16		Inspected 230 horses R.F.A. Made arrangements by referring the Calcium Sulphide a LV.S. & the whole of the horses of B (S.Staff) Battery in the evening.	
	6/6/16		All the morning & afternoon "Saw" horses of B (South Staff) Battery being dressed with Calcium Sulphide. All acted Canule & Mire tags marked with an M and sent to the Base. So the inspection for disinfection. All tarnes wagons re-disinfected. They & Harness kit burnt. The horses & all the Battery marked to be hard ground after being disinfected. Men's clothing withdrawn & disinfected.	
	7/6/16		& fresh clothing issued.	
	8/6/16		Inspected D.A.C. (Seaton B) Right Section (Seabantis A & B) Tenn Mod. Seaton D.A.C. Inspected the horses are in good condition & unfit for hard work. 6 horses sent to M.V. yesterday for debility, and I today in I debility & 2 Lymphatic range. The whole of the movements of this Section require special care & attention & this has been brought	

WAR DIARY or INTELLIGENCE SUMMARY

Army Form C. 2118.

Lt Colonel W. Campbell
C.O. 2/1st. 46th (N. Mid)
Division

June 1916

Place	Date	Hour	Summary of Events and Information	Remarks and references to Appendices
	9/6/16		To the orders of C.R.E. & Divisional Commander. Centre Section – 30 animals out at work & rough exam 5 – picked out for isolation & stopping about head & neck. Having a diagnosis of the slight skin disease they were afraid was Epizootic Lymph. Left Section chiefly wild – Condition satisfactory.	
	10/6/16		Inspected 288th Coy A.S.C. Inspected 1/1st Regt of North British Horse chiefly horses the worst & many sellers. Inspected 1/1st Regt of North British Horse disease. To U.S. Herd & Carr. Tanks & are all present under Vet. Division for Veterinary purposes. Five horses were evacuated for suspected mange on 8/6/16. New cases of tetanus evacuation's suspected of U.V.S. trainer for suspected mange, and one of the staff of Colonel Lord C.G consulting the Reviewer is suspected of having mange & is treated & under special observation. Inspected huts in billets – Lucheux &c.	
	11/6/16		Office Int. & 4th Cav. Regs &c.	
	12/6/16		Office Int. & 4th Cav. Regs &c.	
	13/6/16		Horse transport belonging to F.C. (T.E.) reported this arrival from 1/1st Indian Cavalry Division, and is brought up to the strength of 91. C. (T.E.) 46th (N.Mid.) Division, here is the ride 81st Coy. R.V.C Taylor A.V.C (T.F.) evacuated sick. Inspected transport animals of 138th Infantry Brigade	
	14/6/16		At Sectre Inspected animals for Epizootic of 1/1st Mid. M.T.C. Inspected the ground in an area thought to be the most convenient situated for an Advanced Veterinary Collecting Station. & Consults an Advanced Collecting Station myself proves useful.	

WAR DIARY
or
INTELLIGENCE SUMMARY

Army Form C. 2118.

E. Clough Lieut Colonel
A.D.V.S. 46th (N.M.) Division
June 1916

Place	Date	Hour	Summary of Events and Information	Remarks and references to Appendices
	15/6/16		In the near future, my recommendations on the subject have been laid before the General Staff of the Division. Expected arrivals of D.A.C. (Echelon A) at Grienvent.	
	16/6/16		Expected arrivals of D.A.C. (Echelon B) at Newhavencourt. The animals of the D.A.C. have been working short nights & day for the past month & the weather for the last fortnight has been very wet which has also told on their condition. Many of them a very poor % of them are light.	Many are in very poor condition.
	17/6/16		Expected arrival for inspection at N.V.S. Sergt M. Carbutters (T.F.) rejoined. Saw Major Kentish 7th West Kent Regt Palmateer.	
	18/6/16		Sunday 11 am Ch. "In". 1st line 3rd line - animals inspected Capt. T. Through R.A. (T.F.) + 44 (T.F.) inoculated with Grenda & Tetanus against Johnes anaerobic Grems diseases. Very few deaths. 200 cases (a.o.1) have now been inoculated.	
	19/6/16		Sergeant R. Carbutters (T.F.) reported to gz. 189 to Infantry Brigade. Relieved of the Transport animals of 26 Joint Battalion & Platoons 138th & 139th Infantry Brigade all of which are left & working well.	
	20/6/16		Expected arrivals of 232nd Bde R.F.A. (4 Batteries) - Guns being artillery. Expected arrivals for evacuation at N.V.S. Corps wrote informing this H/b of their duties in the event of sure artery wheretofore being here. In two days my cargo expect being abroad being viewed to A.O.V.	
	21/6/16		Expected arrival a/230 + Gde R.F.A.	
	22/6/16		Expected arrivals of D.A.C. N4 Echelons A + B. Three animals shew a slight improvement since Enlist - The weather has been more genial. Stay here.	

Army Form C. 2118.

WAR DIARY
or
INTELLIGENCE SUMMARY

Army Form C. 2118.

(Erase heading not required.) June 1916

Place	Date	Hour	Summary of Events and Information	Remarks and references to Appendices
	23/6/16		Weekly Conference of Veterinary Officers in the morning. Visited La Bazeque in connection with case of mange in 4 Leicesters Regt. Few were exhibiting suspected symptoms.	
	24/6/16		Inspected animals for exhibition at 11.F.8. Inspected two horses related for suspected skin disease in B (South Staffs) Battery 282nd Bgde R.F.A.	
	25/6/16		Enemy bombs dropped on D+S HQ, one horse of A Squadron North Irish Horse killed by one of them and also at Estaminet near VII Corps HQ. Dump. Inspected horses of B Trench 3rd Army Troops Coy at Warlincourt, found them to be in bad working condition, but many of them looked as though required more feed & food. They were not badly in used or twice quartered, but tired & tight in muscles. Fired & properly cared for they were going to be brought forward to inform if "Recurrent nerves" found referred of them to the Veterinary Section & dealt with them accordingly.	
	26/6/16		Visited HQ's of North Mids Heavy Brigade & found that the 4 Batteries Special Brigade R.F.A. at Gommecourt were away on duty & receiving their Veterinary animals (2 H.96) were away on duty & receiving their inspected animals of 31st 38 Bgde D.T.A. caditors of 4 Bty Battery is satisfactory. Inspected animals for exemptions at 11.F.8. Svery of 18th to 19th of June 1916 were killed by shell fire at Somme. One afternoon of 24/6/16 and one wounded. 3 horses of B.A.C. were killed & 1 wounded by shell fire on night of 25-26 near FONQUEVILLERS.	
	27/6/16		Inspected Section 4 B.A.C. (Totalm B) their animals, only on the whole are the	
	28/6/16		D.A.C. are being worked very hard & the weather & very wet. Lieut Ford & the and Capt T ffer to and hospital the dumping station insufficient saw very muddy & heavy. They animals are looking ill & weary & tired & their attacks up.	

Army Form C. 2118.

WAR DIARY
or
INTELLIGENCE SUMMARY
(Erase heading not required)

St Cloud Meuse Dept
A.D.V.S. 46 - (46th) Division
June 1916

Instructions regarding War Diaries and Intelligence Summaries are contained in F.S. Regs., Part II. and the Staff Manual respectively. Title Pages will be prepared in manuscript.

Place	Date	Hour	Summary of Events and Information	Remarks and references to Appendices
	29/6/16		Inspected No 2 Sectn. D.A.C. Mules fairly good — Harness shewing the effects of the bad weather & the difficulty at most of these Units as they would pull and grease favourable weather permitting & not too hard work — They are working very hard at present. D.D.V.S. 3rd Army inspected animals labored for Casting sg. for mange "other than the trenches" at A.V.S. 28 animals were rested up DOR for evacuation to Rouen for "mange", various "mount mange". A.V.S. evacuated 20 sick horses, and 23 animals cast for "recurrent mange" by D.D.V. 3rd Army. Weekly Conference of I.O.s. Two animals cast. Flew killed by shell fire during the past week. No wounded during same period.	
	30/6/16			

W.M. Bryant
A.D.V.S. St Cloud
A.D.V.S. 46 - (46th) Division

Secret

Headquarters
46th Division

War Diaries of A.D.V.S. 46th Division
& O.C. 1/1 N. Midld. Mobile Veterinary Section for July 1916
are forwarded herewith.

M. MacDougall
Lt. Colonel
A.D.V.S. 46th Division

Army Form C. 2118.

WAR DIARY (Lansborough 2nd & 46th (N. Mid) Division)
INTELLIGENCE SUMMARY

(Erase heading not required.)

July 1916.

Place	Date	Hour	Summary of Events and Information	Remarks and references to Appendices
Pas	2/7/16		Inspected animals for evacuation at N.V.S.	
"	3/7/16		Went to Barvincourt to arrange with O.D.V.S. 37th Division about fitting over his billets & billets for N.V.S. as their Division is moving into their Brig: trenches.	
"	4/7/16		O.i/c N.V.S. nurned from Pas to BAVINCOURT.	
"	5/7/16		Inspected new billets of 1/1st Field N.V.S. at BAVINCOURT.	
"	6/7/16		Major General the Hon'ble E.J. Montague-Stuart-Wortley C.B., C.M.G., M.V.O., D.S.O. relinquished Command of 46th (N. Mid'd) Divn & visited N.V.S. enroute to Hdqrs at Larbret. Inspected animals of Divisional Headquarters, Signal Coy R.E. and this Troop of A Squadron North Irish Horse. Nightly Expenses of Veterinary Officer. Inspected animals for evacuation at N.V.S.	
"	7/7/16		Inspected 6 isolated animals of "Echelon B" D.A.C.	
"	8/7/16		Visit of Tobby sent back to 4th Cavalry Regt from N.V.S. in accordance with Order of D.A.Q.G. 3rd Echelon who stated that this man's Transfer to 1/2nd N Mid M.T. was not in order as the two Commanders had not the power to sanction it. The D.A.Q.G 3rd Echelon has been asked to sanction it if not has then returned to 4 Cav Reg. Founding Mortuaries.	

249 Wt. W14957/M90 750,000 1/16 J.B.C. & A. Forms/C.2118/12.

WAR DIARY or INTELLIGENCE SUMMARY

Army Form C. 2118.

(Erase heading not required.)

St. Glass Wagon Dumps
A.D.V.S. 46th Division
July 1916

Place	Date	Hour	Summary of Events and Information	Remarks and references to Appendices
"	10/7/16		Inspected No. 3 Section D.A.C. for Mange. The Sarcoptic was found on a horse of this Section yesterday.	
"	11/7/16		Inspected animals for evacuation at M.V.S. & advanced Clearing Post. Inspected all animals of Echelon B. D.A.C. for skin disease along with V.O. I/c (Captain Wortley)	
"	12/7/16		44 animals were evacuated today by 1st & 3rd M.V.S. 24 of which were Mange or Suspected Mange. 4 x belonged to Ambulances the 46th Division of which 5 were Mange or Suspected Mange. 15 of the Mange cases were from the D.A.C. - Captain T. Nangro A.V.C. (T.F.) has been attached for temporary duty attacking to the D.A.C. as a temporary measure. Will strenuously try to deal with the Mange in that Unit, & to try to bring the & raise the standard of workmanship generally in that Unit.	
"	13/7/16		Inspected all the Batteries of 231st and 232nd Brigades R.F.A. at Monchiet.	
"	14/7/16		Twenty Conference of A.D's.	
"	15/7/16		Inspected animals for evacuation at M.V.S. Inspected the Batteries of 230th Bgde R.F.A.	
"	16/7/16		Visit to No. 3 Section D.A.C. regarding another which are being taken to check refused of mange	

War Diary or Intelligence Summary

Army Form C. 2118.

Lt. Colonel W.M. McDougall
D.A.D.V.S. 46 Div. North Midland

Place	Date	Hour	Summary of Events and Information	Remarks and references to Appendices
"	17/7/16		Inspected some suspected skin cases at M.V.S. also inspected advanced Veterinary Collecting Post.	
"	18/7/16		Inspected horses (sick) of 232nd Brigade R.F.A., 3rd Midland Field Ambulance, 138th Infantry Brigade. Inspected animals for evacuation at M.V.S. in the afternoon.	
"	19/7/16		Inspected 90 remounts at O.R.C. which were being distributed to units of the Division. Director of Veterinary Services, D.D.V.S. 3rd Army visited the Division. All officers R.A.V.C. (T.F.) attached at my offices to meet the Director who advised them in several points – full chiefly on the subject of Manage. D.V.S. inspected M.V.S. at Souvamp Farms.	
"	20/7/16		Inspected animals of 1st and 2nd N. Midland Field Ambulances.	
"	21/7/16		Held Enquiry of V.O.s Inspected animals for evacuation at M.V.S.	
"	22/7/16		Inspected No 1 Section D.A.C. – Divisional Signal Coy R.E. and D.H.Q.	
"	23/7/16		Inspected animals for evacuation at M.V.S.	
"	24/7/16		VIIth Corps Commander inspected horses of 231st Brigade R.F.A.; C Battery 232nd Brigade; A, B, and C Batteries 233rd Brigade R.F.A. The Divisional Commander & D Branch of the Staff were present. I also attended.	

WAR DIARY or INTELLIGENCE SUMMARY

Army Form C. 2118.

July 1916. Lt. Colonel W. Gray Bryand
A.D.V.S. 26th Division

Place	Date	Hour	Summary of Events and Information	Remarks and references to Appendices
"	25/7/16.		VIIth Corps Commander inspected animals of A & B Batteries 233rd Brigade R.F.A. and D.A.C. The condition of the animals was considered satisfactory. B Battery 233rd Bde had in very poor condition. A Battery was satisfactory, and the mules of D.A.C. were effected the Batteries respectively during the last two weeks. Horses have improved considerably during the last two weeks. The Div. Commander, C.R.A., A.Q. & Q.M.G., & A.D.V.S. attended the Corps Commander's inspection. Inspected all four Batteries of the D.A.C. the morning & tested a general improvement everywhere at this visit. Captain Thorney R.A.V.C.(T.F.) has done a great deal towards improving the "workmanship" of this Unit & to prevent entailing mange. A great deal still remains to be done but good progress has been made.	
"	26/7/16.		Inspected animals for evacuation at M.V.S. 233rd Brigade & R.F.A. certain cases in conjunction with the V.O. in charge.	
"	27/7/16.		Visited M.V.S.	
"	28/7/16.		Inspected Echelon B (1st & 4th Sections) D.A.C. Animals have improved in condition & the horses have been washed with Crude resulto inclusiv with sulphur. Subside of Jar of emptinginus cases are involved pursuing a definite action — to which they have mange or not. 230th Bgde R.F.A. Sports.	
"	29/7/16.		Inspected animals of Divl. W.G.M.G., 230th Bgde R.F.A. Sports.	

WAR DIARY
or
INTELLIGENCE SUMMARY

Army Form C. 2118.

Place	Date	Hour	Summary of Events and Information	Remarks and references to Appendices
"	31/7/16		Reported arrivals for evacuation at M.V.S. & Advanced Collecting Pk. Circulated against diseases. Every Officer, N.C.O, & man of the Army Veterinary Corps serving with the B.A.V.S. has been circulated against Typhoid & Paratyphoid disease by this R.A.M.C. with the most recent protectes vaccine imp a mixed vaccine affording protection against Typhoid & Para-typhoid. As the circulars thus usefully conducing a little explanation is further necessary in these case.	N. Cours MacDougall A.D.V.S. 46-(N. Midland) [signature] N. MacDougall S. Colonel A.D.V.S. 46-(N.Midland) Division.

MEMORANDUM.

Army Form C. 348.

From A.D.M.S.

To A.D.V.S. 46th Division

No. 3/420
Date 28-7-16
A.D.M.S. 46th (N. MID.) DIV. T.F.

July 28 1916.

Will you please convey to the officers and men under your command our high appreciation of the esprit de corps shown by them in having attained such a high percentage of inoculation against disease — We beg also to thank you for your example and administrative assistance. Such spirit proves a satisfactory state of interior economy

W Lee ?? Col. A.D.M.S. 46th Division

ANSWER.

191 .

O.C. 1/1st N. Mid. M.V.S.

Forwarded for your information. The A.D.M.S.'s appreciation should I think be communicated to the N.C.O.s & men. Kindly return.

MacDougall
Lt-Colonel
A.D.V.S. 46th Div.
28/7/16

1688/16
28/7/16

P.T.O

(3)

To
A.D.V.S
46ᵀᴴ Divsn

Returned to you, please.
It is very gratifying
to think that the M.V.S.
has deserved this
commendation

C Hartley
Capt. A.V.C
1/1ˢᵗ N.M.M.V.S
46ᵀᴴ Div

29/VII/16

Note

(1) 100 per cent of 1/1ˢᵗ N.
Midland M.V.S. inoculated
also

(2) 100 per cent of Officers
A.V.C. & Sergeants
A.V.C. attached to
Units of the Division

McDougall
Lt Colonel
A.D.V.S. 46ᵀᴴ Division

A.D.V.S.

16th Division

10/14
Aug

WAR DIARY or INTELLIGENCE SUMMARY

Army Form C. 2118.

of A. Col. Vans-Agnew 1st A.D.M.S. 46th (N. Mid) Division
(August 1916) 1st Sheet

Place	Date	Hour	Summary of Events and Information	Remarks and references to Appendices
BAVINCOURT	1st August		41st F. Mid. M.A.S. evacuated 18 cwsual & of Divnal & attached Units and 3 arrivals of other units. Total 21.	
	2nd		Expected arrival of D.A.G. with Captain T. Tomer, A.V.C. (T.F.) The change over to be in hand. All strongly effects animals sans peur evacuated & the remaining strong healthy animals have been dinned with Eleven Rifles (Warner Saddlers Saddlery &c) has been inspected. Captain T. Tomer has been ordered to rejoin the 230th Brigade R.F.A. on Monday 7/8/16.	
	3rd			
	4th		Weekly Conference of M.O.s at my Office. Inspected animals for evacuation at Advanced Collecting Post & at M.V.S.	
	5th		Inspected horses of Divnl HQrs & Signal Coy R.E.	
	6th		Inspected horses of 230th Bgde R.F.A. Lectured to Officers & N.C.O.s at Bavincourt on 230th Bde R.F.A. Lines.	
	7th		Inspected horses of 231st Bgde R.F.A. Lectured to Officers & N.C.O.s at MONCHIET in Lines of 231st Bgde R.F.A.	
	8th		Inspected animals for evacuation at M.V.S. and Advanced Collecting P.t.	
	9th		R.O. 1/S 3rd Army inspected B C & D Batteries 230th Bgde R.F.A.	
	10th		2, 3 & 4 Sections (b) A.G. A, B & C Batteries 231st Bgde R.F.A.	
	11th		No. 1, 9th 3rd Army inspected 231st Bgde R.F.A. A, B, C, D Batteries & A Battery 232nd Bgde R.F.A. 85 Yd. Batteries 233rd Bgde R.F.A. & A Battery 231st Bgde R.F.A. No. 1 Section 2/1st N. Mid. Park.	

WAR DIARY or INTELLIGENCE SUMMARY

Army Form C. 2118.

(Erase heading not required.)

G. S. Branch H.Q. 48th (W.M.) Division
2nd Sheet

Place	Date	Hour	Summary of Events and Information	Remarks and references to Appendices
	11th Aug		Weekly Conference of C.O.s	
	12th "		230th Bgde R.F.A. Inspected at La Royere Farm.	
	13th "		Inspected area of H.Q.	
	13th "		D.D.T.S. 2nd Army inspected A Battery 230th Bgde R.F.A. Calvaire Dorp H.Q.S. 1st 2nd & 3rd Field Ambulances – H.Q.S. – 454th, by A.D.S. – 1st 2nd & 3rd Auto-M.G. Field Cos R.E. – 1st Mammoth Rgt –	
	14th "		2nd/1st 1st 2nd & 3rd 137th Infantry Brigade Transport	
			137th Infantry Brigade Transport. Visited Corbie Stations & rail Inspected equipment expectation of H.Q.S. arriving & dividing their Equip 7. Neuruns but by then new lot of arriving Individuals their Transport was attd to the rest	
	16th "		Formers was attd to Transport	
			Weekly Conference of C.O.s Went by Motor to Forum of Thiaux Formin Lorries to investigate as to what fires & tent lorry had died of during last winter defts & repair. 10th Ambulance & Div. 2nd Army rgt had several cases of Swine Fowling recently, the Vets reported that war transport egg & Manure tyfird days visited Vendelment Sap leads into to the Employees who worked there. Inspected animals for evacuation of H.Q.S.	
	19th "		Horse show of 139th Infantry Brigade at BAILLEUVAL - judged	
	20th "		the jumping.	
			Lectured at 6th Army Battery School at HAUTECLOQUE Reserve Feet	
	21st "		D.D.T.S. 2nd Army Gen. Staff	

Army Form C. 2118.

WAR DIARY
of Lt Colonel ~~Intelligence~~ A.D.V.S. 46-(N.Mid) Division
INTELLIGENCE SUMMARY
3rd Chap
(Erase heading not required.)

Instructions regarding War Diaries and Intelligence Summaries are contained in F. S. Regs., Part II. and the Staff Manual respectively. Title Pages will be prepared in manuscript.

Place	Date	Hour	Summary of Events and Information	Remarks and references to Appendices
	22/8/16		Inspected animals of No 1 Section D.A.C. at LE GROS TISON Farm. V.O. having reported several cases of suspected mange. 3 animals are being sent to U.V.S. for observation, & a 4th to animals of the Section are going to be inspected with a view to segregating suspects of pre-war army Calvens sale. Ainmais mspected of pre-war army animals. Nil 1.O., has been in force for animals in this Section from Nil 1.O., until of the Division.	
	23/8/16		Inspected animals at advanced Veterinary Collecting Station LARBRET.	
	24/8/16		Inspected animals for eventing at M.F.S.	
	25/8/16		Weekly Conference of V.O's. Visit to D.A.C. & A.C.S. trenches transport (74 Horses and 1 Mule) prior to their being distributed to units. They were inspected by Captain T. Kennedy M.R.S.(I.F.) on detrainment at SAULTY Station. The inspection of remounts in as far as if frequent means that the V.O. has to travel at the station for 6 to 7 hours of a day, & he every (?evening) arrangement has been made for informing him half a day of the V.O.'s time to keep them waiting at the Station. They be current river arms & time is wasted. The fact of remounts being Divisioned on the railway they being furnished these them direct to Units at the station setting some relief is coming out in a caused delay in getting our remounts off the train.	

WAR DIARY
of Lt. Colonel Macdougall A.D.V.S 46th Field Division
or
INTELLIGENCE SUMMARY
(Erase heading not required.)
(August 1916) 4th Sheet

Army. Form C. 2118.

Instructions regarding War Diaries and Intelligence Summaries are contained in F. S. Regs., Part II. and the Staff Manual respectively. Title Pages will be prepared in manuscript.

Place	Date	Hour	Summary of Events and Information	Remarks and references to Appendices
	26/8/16		No 1 W. Med. M.V.S. moved from SONCAMP FARM to L'ARBRET.	
	27/8/16		Inspected Signal Coy R.E. and Div HdQ animals.	
	28/8/16		Inspected "A" "B" "C" & "D" Batteries 231st Bgde R.F.A at MONCHIET and the horses of all these Batteries have improved in condition. 4 or 5 horses are segregated in C Battery but they show no definite signs of mange. Two are segregated in D Battery one of which is a remount which joined 4 weeks ago. None are segregated in the other two Batteries. All segregated horses have been dressed with Calcium Sulphide. And all the horses of A & C Batteries have been washed with Calcium Sulphide. Inspected horses of A Battery 232nd Bgde R.F.A at MONCHIET, they are in good condition & there are no segregated horses. Inspected horses of A & B Batteries 233rd Bgde R.F.A at LA BAZEQUE Farm. Condition of both these Batteries is satisfactory. B. Battery horses were poor a little time ago but they have now improved and are in fairly good condition. Two remounts which joined A Batty 4 days ago are segregated & their skins are suspicious of Sarcoptic Mange but it is thought that one or two dressings with Calcium Sulphide will put them right. The 233rd Bgde R.F.A. will cease to exist tomorrow on reorganisation of the Divl Artillery. 1st Batteries going to 230th Bgde & 1st Batteries going to the 231st Bgde. Captains J.A.D. Harvey A. V. C. [?] attached to 233rd Bgde has been ordered to join the B.A.C. when 233rd Bgde	

WAR DIARY / INTELLIGENCE SUMMARY

Army Form C. 2118.

of **A. Cav: of Auxill: Brigade A.V.C. 46th (N.M.) Division**
(August 1916) 5th Sheet

Place	Date	Hour	Summary of Events and Information	Remarks and references to Appendices
	29/8/16		Cleans & Exect. Sergeant Ellis Cyples & Driver A.V.C. (T) at present attached to 1 B & C. Batteries 233rd Bde. inspected on Exf. by the M.V.S. traversed sanitary practice of these Batteries. C. Battery 233rd - Except that at rear of the lines there is no satisfactory lines made but the horses of this section are situated & grazed above any noxious exposure of house.	
	30/8/16		Visited M.V.S. Ellis Captain New Town Aux D duties to the East with two arrival port. Inspected 56 horses along with Capt Hartney O.C. A.V.D 46th Div. at SHAWTY Station.	O.B.R. 3rd Army
	31/8/16		Inspected transport animals of 139th Infantry Brigade at BAILLEUL R.S. Visited Captain New Town Aux D (T) who said he paid a visit to T Filliot Farbarieur.	

W.W. Bryant Lt. Colonel
A.V.C. 46th (N. Mid) Division

W.W. Bryant Lt. Colonel
A.V.C. 46th (N. Mid) Division.

War Diary.
September 1916.

A.D.V.S.
46th Div.

Army Form C. 2118.

WAR DIARY or INTELLIGENCE SUMMARY

of Lt Colonel M.W. O'Donnell, A.D.M.S 46th (N. Midl.) Division
(September 1916) — Sheet

Vol 15

Place	Date	Hour	Summary of Events and Information	Remarks and references to Appendices
BAVINCOURT	1/9/16		Weekly Conference of M.O.'s Inspected 1/3rd D. Watters 232nd Bgde R.F.A. at "LA CAUCHIE". M.O's evacuated to Amiens 5 F.A. 23 Base Hospital. 15 Tones of North End Mixture attached to M.U. of 46th Divn were inoculated with Vaccine by Capt C. Martin R.V.C. (T.F.)	
	2/9/16		Inspected the 15 Tones of St. Marie inoculated yesterday & unobserved any signs of reaction. Inspected H.P. 4 Sector of 46th Div.	
	3/9/16		Inspected the 16 Tones of N.T.H attached to M.U.G. of 46th Divn to master. Capt C. Martin R.V.C. (T.F.) inoculated four Tones of S.A.A attached to 46th Divn. (Signalling School) — West-Mallelio	
	4/9/16		Attended Conference at M.Q. 2.30 – 4.30 P.M. Inspected the annual post evacuation of M.U.S. Visits Cubicular few Fever Cure (T.F.) who were ill in H.P.1. 21 Ambulances. Inspected sub-Cures of Cubicular incubated with Fuitin Furstrin. To reactor	
	5/9/16		Inspected Surplus Tropes of Divisional Artillery — 48 wolf — 110 which were sent to M.U.S. an Veterinary safety. 2 Cuts were sent back to D. Battery 232 — Bgd facant instructed as to carting to other units of the Division. 31 Tones their remainder in the Waggon for Carrying Self & Supplies two were returned to cure	

WAR DIARY
or
INTELLIGENCE SUMMARY

Lt Colonel Maurice Byfield A.D.V.S.
2nd Corps 46th Div.
September 1916.

Army Form C. 2118.

Place	Date	Hour	Summary of Events and Information	Remarks and references to Appendices

			230th Bgde Others - L.D.
			 A Battery = 1 2
			 B " = 6 —
			 C " = — —
			 D " = 3 —
			              9 2 = Total 11
			
			 232nd Bgde
			 A Battery = 6 —
			 B " = — —
			 C " = 3 1
			 D " = — —
			              9 1 = Total 20
			                      31
			
			 233rd Bgde
			 B Battery = 5 horses
			 C " = 1 "
			
			 232nd Bgde
			 A Battery = 4 horses
			 D " = 1 "
			              11
				Surplus stock Transfer to Reinforcement Depot.
				
				 Sent to U.V.S. for evacuation on Rly. Cases.
				
				 These L.D. animals returned to D. Pot. = 2B.3D
				 Bgds. sent'g Transfer to 186th Inf'y Bgde.
				              31
				              11
				              3
				 Total 45
				 45 was the total number of Surplus horses in excess to Origin't Est'ty.

2449   Wt. W14957/M90   750,000   1/16   J.B.C. & A.   Forms/C.2118/12.

WAR DIARY
or
INTELLIGENCE SUMMARY

Army Form C. 2118.

of Lt-Colonel Wm Bryant A.D.V.S.
46th Division
September 1916

Place	Date	Hour	Summary of Events and Information	Remarks and references to Appendices
	6/9/16.		Inspected animals for evacuation at M.V.S. Capt Murphy F.A.V.C. (T.F.) returned to duty from sick list, & joined the D.A.C. for duty.	
	7/9/16.		Inspected horses of D. C.+ D. Batteries & O.C D.A.C.	
	8/9/16.		D.A.D.V.S. Army inspected surplus horses of R.Q. also animals for Vice + Staff Remount reserve. The animals arrived at BAVINCOURT. These reached in inspecting them from 9.30 A.M. to 1 P.M. and store belonging to the 46th Div were sent direct to their units — to be seen by D.D.V.S. in daylight next day.	
	9/9/16.		Inspected animals at M.V.S. (afternoon) for evacuation. Inspected No.4 Section D.A.C. of D.A.C. for a few min. & saw 60 of their wagons and about 30 mile stream which appear they would grant of their horses which do not look like ringworm & they would wish to get on the animals would appear to have something to with their covering out flesh in their cut square trouble. Capt Rees Roberts (T.F.) is in Veterinary charge of the evening until No. 4 Section.	
	10/9/16		No condition & duting with it.	
	11/9/16		Had "Redwing" & "Scipi" shot with "tib" in front. Went to M.V.S. in morning. Attended 138th Infantry Bde Sports in afternoon. Brig.Gen Rolfe-Hambling "Crip"(wounded).	
	12/9/16.		Visited Horse Show & Gymkhana of 137 I.B. Inspected horses of D. Battery in evening.	

WAR DIARY or INTELLIGENCE SUMMARY

Army Form C. 2118.

(Erase heading not required.)

Lt. Colonel MacDonald R.A.M.C.
A.D.M.S. 47th Division
September 1916.

Place	Date	Hour	Summary of Events and Information	Remarks and references to Appendices
	12/9/16 (cont.)		1/1st S. Mid. M.F.A. evacuated 49 animals for "Revernt [Recurrent] Mange" – 57 were on D.D.R.s list but two others belonging to the Divl. Artillery were not sent to the M.F.S.	
	13/9/16		Inspected A/B Batteries 233rd Bgde R.F.A. at La Couché's. Investigated the cause of death of two Gr.s. belonging to M/2 Cresst [?] Farmers Barracks along with Capt. Stear Orderlieut. A.D.M.S. (?) who had reported that they died of lead poisoning owing to the fact the men had drunk water which was [kept] exposed in the field in tubs they primed by the 149th Army Troops Coy R.E. B'pont & tot. 141st Army Troops Coy R.E. B'pont on this subject was forwarded & 46th Divl. Hd.Qrs. by Capt Ormulistair [?] his report — a forwarding circuit by A.D.M.S. Inspected No.3 Sectn. 46th O.A.S. and Rect. Res. Fd. Ambulances.	
	14/9/16		Inspected animals for evacuation at M.F.S. in the afternoon.	
	15/9/16		Medically Inspected men of F.Bs. Inspected horses of A.V.B. & tot. cor. 2307 Bgde R.F.A.	
	16/9/16		Conducted inspection of A Battery 233rd Bgde R.F.A. Horses greatly improved & all are now in good condition.	

2449 Wt. W14957/M90 750,000 1/16 J.B.C. & A. Forms/C.2118/12.

Army Form C. 2118.

WAR DIARY or INTELLIGENCE SUMMARY

of Lt Colonel W.A.M. Duncall D.S.O.
2nd Sheep
September 1916.

(Erase heading not required.)

Place	Date	Hour	Summary of Events and Information	Remarks and references to Appendices
	14/9/16.		Inspected 2nd/1st Mgt James & 2nd/1st Sigurd Coy. Reported animals for evacuation at A.V.S.	
	18/9/16.		Attended a Conference at VIIth Corps H.Qrs. to discuss "Proposals for the Control of Mange". There were present Brig-General W. Cattley, the VIIth Corps, Lt. Colnel W.A.M. Duncall A.D.V.S. 46th Divn., Major Neale A.D.V.S. 17th Divn. (V.O. i/c to 19th Divn.), Major Runtlitt A.D.V.S. 33rd Divn, Major Duffy V.O. i/c to 2nd Corps & Captain Statfield R.E. VIIth Corps. The trunks discussed were three dealt with by the Director of Veterinary Services in his recent memorandum, to provide a Cadium Sulphide bath in the Corps area by the Corps principally assisted about, have the clipping about their end of October (horses & mules to be clipped 2 once except the legs. The treatment recommended to work the P.C.B. by the P.C.B. & the double P.C.B. Bettony scrub) one medalia (for mange) & the new on the double to Bettony scrub not be required to supply any of the treatment, as H.Q. to see how this must cannot be carried. I rained hard all day.	
	19/9/16.		Visited SOMBRIN which is now in our 2nd Line area about 5/8 and 4 Sections R.A.C. are housed this, also Div. Supply Column. COUTURELLE handed over to units of our 46th Divn. and the 1st & 2nd J. Mid Field Ambulances which were billeted there are being moved to BAVINCOURT and MONDICOURT respectively. Both were inspected and found very very much, were staying at COUTURE & Hd., Sigd. D. Batteries 261st Bgd R.F.A. D. Batteries 281st Bgd R.F.A.	
	20/9/16.			

WAR DIARY
or
INTELLIGENCE SUMMARY of 1st Cav.(?) Div. Mobile Vet. Sec. A.V.C.
September 1916.
6th Sheet

Army Form C. 2118.

Place	Date	Hour	Summary of Events and Information	Remarks and references to Appendices
	22/9/16		Weekly Conference of V.O.s Inspected A B + D Batteries 232nd Bgde R.F.A.	
	23/9/16		Inspected animals for evacuation at M.V.S.	
	24/9/16		Inspected No.3 Section D.A.C. The condition of the animals of this Section has improved. The "Cryptions" (?) ringworm referred to on 9/9/16 as existing in No.4 Section only a few cases seemed unwilling to treatment. Many of the cases were thought by the O.C. Unit to be ringworm were I think simply "Abolicis"(?) caused by the sand, at all events they recovered without treatment the hair growing again on the bare patches. Two bare patches were often about size of walnut.	
	25/9/16		Guess. VII Corps Races at LA BAZEQUE in the afternoon	
	26/9/16		Marched to ABBEVILLE with Captain C. Claverty(?) near the Cairum(?) Substitute Bath at No.5 Veterinary Hospital of use. Also interviewed the D.V.S.	
	27/9/16		Inspected transport animals of 137th Infantry Bgde. & 1/2 Field Coy. R.E. Also inspected animals for evacuation to M.V.S.	
	28/9/16		Inspected No.3 Section D.A.C. at Gardiempré, & 230th Bgde R.F.A. at HENU.	

WAR DIARY or INTELLIGENCE SUMMARY

Army Form C. 2118.

September 1916 4th Sheet

Place	Date	Hour	Summary of Events and Information	Remarks and references to Appendices
	29/9/16		Inspected animals of F.4 Section (Echelon B), 46th D.A.C. at WARLINCOURT in afternoon. Weekly Conferences of F.O.'s in the evening.	
	30/9/16		Inspected B.C. and D. Batteries 232nd Bde R.F.A. at MONCHIET. The horses of this Brigade have improved in condition, for the W.O.C. is put satisfactory. All the animals of the Divisional Artillery Lines in general in condition & they are good on the whole. Satisfactory. They have been to tie carts for cart of late, the experience thus of grooming as been better & change in battery next to effect. One Inspected case from B.230 that executed last week tried in that only case verified as reserved for several weeks.	

M.W. Dougall Lt. Colonel
C.O. J. S. 46th (N. Md.) Division

A.M. Dougall Lt. Colonel
A.D.V.S. 46th N. Md. Division

A. McQuarrie Lt.
46th Division
Forwarded

A.M. Dougall Lt. Colonel
A.D.V.S. 46th N. Md. Division

Secret

Headquarters
46th Division.

Herewith War Diaries of A.D.V.S.
46th Division, and S.C. 1/1st North
Midland Mobile Veterinary Section for
month of October 1916, for favour of
disposal.

M.MacDougall
Lt. Colonel
A.D.V.S. 46th (N.Mid) Division

3/11/16

WAR DIARY
INTELLIGENCE SUMMARY of 1st Field Veterinary Sec. A.V.C. 46th Div.
October 1916. 1st Sheet

Army Form C. 2118.

Place	Date	Hour	Summary of Events and Information	Remarks and references to Appendices
BAVINCOURT	1/10/16		Expected arrivals of Div. M.Offrs and Officers Cdg R.E.	
	3/10/16		Expected tours of Nos 1 Section 3/1st London Fd. Hy 18 & relieving more suffering from Fever of all Influenza type. Forwarded sailing reports to D.D.V.S. Army & Brig. Commander the the fever which is circulated amongst the horses of various units of the Divn. Viz:—	
			No. 1 Section 24th Reserve Park A.S.C. = 18 Cases	
			230 th Bgde R.F.A. = 16 cases	
			231 st Bgde R.F.A. = 8 "	
			451 st Coy A.S.C. = 6 "	
			Signal Coy R.E. = 3 "	
			51	
			Captain New Fraser R.A.V.C. (T.F.)	
	4/10/16		Three (3) CAUSALTY LAZARET Section. To cross from Boulogne on 5/10/16 & 4.30 P.M. train. Successor has been appointed as Veterinary Officer of the D.A.C. during Captain Fraser's absence. Total cases of Influenza in the Division (51)	
	5/10/16		D.D.V.S. 3rd Army inspected the fever cases of 451st Coy A.S.C. with the Vet in charge - cases of 232nd Bgde R.F.A. to visit visiting to D.V.S.	
	6/10/16		Expected 9 horses of B/233 Bgd R.F.A. at M.V.S. noted Coy 2 as suspected rough interred the tag tay of fifty pattern to be clipped to followed quickly with a serum solution tight wings immersed, followed by weak carbolic following out did restore- ling desired completion.	

WAR DIARY
or
INTELLIGENCE SUMMARY

Army Form C. 2118.

Place	Date	Hour	Summary of Events and Information	Remarks and references to Appendices
BAVINCOURT	6/10/16		Usually Occurrences of V.D's – Cases of Influenza in Division 98. Inspected horses of 1st Field Amb. R.E. at N.U.S. remounted lines.	
"	7/10/16		Inspected horses along Ponches. Turning of Cases of Influenza.	
"	8/10/16		Inspected horses of Divn 1 F. Amb, 1/8/232 Sept R.T.B. 22 Sanitary Section Visits to 91st Battn at R416 ... Cases of Influenza in Division 96. Visited Lt. Col. Mann A.D.V.S. 47th (2nd) Division at OUTRELLE.	
"	9/10/16		Inspected horse lines of 1/8/232 Sept R.T.B. at LA CAUCHIE vm Tones which had been allotted for Veterinary Reserve.	
"	10/10/16		...	

WAR DIARY or INTELLIGENCE SUMMARY

Army Form C. 2118.

of Lt-Colonel W.W.O. Beveridge
October 1916   3rd Sheet

Place	Date	Hour	Summary of Events and Information	Remarks and references to Appendices
BAVINCOURT	10/10/16	cont	The Influenza attacks of the Horses is disappearing & many of the cases have been cured. The Horses are pretty well off for about 8 days & after that rapidly improving although in some cases they rapidly lose stability there is especially so in those cases where the Nervous weaknesses are relative. The treatment in cases where the Nervous symptoms are evoked returns some of the Horses to — has an Elixir &c. filtered & given to them of Magnesium Sulphate. 30% The W.O. are all yellow & mighty injected & so is that in some instances. The race key & strong arising later of Mag. Sulph: Levice in weak there fails to aid. acute state Puerto Logo of Strychnine is used. The symptoms of the cases of Influenza which we have had are:— Cough & Pullulg. Temperature 103° to 106°. dull & heavy & tired, eyes closed discharge of tears, W.U. injected, & apetite lost, has feet affected &c. & some cases as the U.S. follow. There are No dead. The worst cases Reports to 7 to 8 days, the with merely Fever symptoms may return.	
	11/10/16		None not seen effected on this outbreak	
	12/10/16		Inspected the lines of Horse lines of No. 3 Section D.A.C. the condition was very injurious especially mud & dirt & in process of becoming worse, 11 N.S.O. by order of B.G.R.A. Returns 2nd & 3rd Regt R.F.A. of Manch. C.F.T. have Q.R.M.S. orders were issued cover in Stalls to which Horse Feed.	

Army Form C. 2118.

WAR DIARY
or
INTELLIGENCE SUMMARY

(Erase heading not required.)

of Lt Colonel Macdonnell
October 1916 — 1st Sheet

Army Form C. 2118.

Place	Date	Hour	Summary of Events and Information	Remarks and references to Appendices
BAIZIEUX	12/10/16		Wrote to M.O's of Brigades Field Ambulance & A.V.C. (T.F.) also attached asking that Nominal Rolls may be submitted for F.S. Post Cards of those R.E. O's in accordance with P.O. 84/6/1914 dated E.N.G. 11/10/16.	
"	13/10/16		Weekly Employ of 8.T.P. Sent forward for 14/4/- to Sergt. Seward & M/ess C.B. D.F.S. B.S. Photograph of M/jor M.G.O. of No. 28 C.E.C (T.F.) 46 - (North) Division to the Hon Kitchener National Memorial Fund. Incidents arrived for evacuation of N.L.S. & A Section (M) 15. N.C.O, 34 L.C, 5 R.F.A. 5 Muls arrived at SAULTY LARRET Station from DIEPPE. They were inspected by Captain F. Armitstead, O.N.C.(T.F.) & found to be free from Glanders & others diseases. The N.A.C. were sent to abide with the Battery for the duration of the war.	
"	14/10/16		Arrived strength of Post 4 P.M. Embarked aircraft of Lewis of A B & D batteries 2/33rd Bgde R.F.A. at LA CAUCHIE. Condition satisfactory. A Battery special contribution to the likes as this unit has not yet got suppl of tripods for guns.	
"	15/10/16		Weather Steaming. Shod New Tractors (T.F.) returned from Corps Ambulance Pvt. 11497 Lewis & Gifford Corp R.E.	

Army Form C. 2118.

WAR DIARY
or
INTELLIGENCE SUMMARY

Lt-Colonel Newbrugh
October 1916.   6th Sheet

(Erase heading not required.)

Place	Date	Hour	Summary of Events and Information	Remarks and references to Appendices
BAVINCOURT	16/10/16.		Inspected animals for evacuation at N.U.V.S. Inspected animals sick of 1st & 3rd N. Mid. Field Ambulances at GOUY-EN-ARTOIS.	
"	17/10/16.		Inspected animals for evacuation at N.U.V.S. (These admitted since the inspection yesterday). Inspected 1st Lieut D.A.C. - Condition satisfactory. Some of the men are not in every etarding at night. Remainder have view are put in every standing by themselves, to stand outside. To inspect motived. No profit motived by the Division for over this week. Fear are of any kind & the units are unfunded as for as the truth standing & such huts are without not being available. Head cover to be turned owing to nothing not being available. Instructions for the Division use are due at SAULTY - ABBETER 4 P.M. I will tried to see them but they were led & not likely to arrive in daylight. They are being inspected by Capt. Fair faces R/A(T) & at the D.A.C. before proceeding at 9 A.M. Transport Six heart cars of highways have been examined viz. 283 Field R.F.A. 1A Batty = 3 B " = 2 C " = 1 = 6 1st Monmouth Regt	

WAR DIARY
INTELLIGENCE SUMMARY

Army Form C. 2118.

(Erase heading not required.)

Month: October 1916

Place	Date	Hour	Summary of Events and Information	Remarks and references to Appendices
BAYONCOURT	18/10/16		Inspected arrivals of 138th Infantry Regt. The 5th Reserve Regt. and 5th Leicestershire Regt. had their arrivals inspected in the Place Sabrage. The 4th Leicester & 4th Lincoln Regts are in the Place. They are a C looking lot. 34 Runny inspected officers of Regts in the billets 1/6 to 1/87th Infantry Regt of Edinburgh.	
	19/10/16		O.C. inspected 1st Bn. K.R.9.1.4 of 187. Motor Bys G of Edinburgh 137th and 139th Infantry Bdes cancelled on account of Witt weather. Ry/ach at off. Rode to Manchester York - By D Battery (2 E F) Bde R.F.A. officers were active, but it was, the lives at Enquéule.	
	20/10/16		O.O.C. inspected 1st, 2nd & 1st line Transport of 138th Infantry Bde. 1st Monmouths Regt. - One tty of A.S.C, towing the people. Netty defence of the Bn. officers, but gave it received orders to hand its 8 OC, inspector of Transport.	
	21/10/16		Inspected an application for execution CHUS.	
	20/10/16		Dispatched by Post Dublicate copies of my War Diary for dated from 31st August 1914 to 30th September 1916 to officers in charge BTO. Peertho Bros. 18. 8. Ty. Pts for safe custody until after the War. Forwarded copies of Bn. K. 9.24 of Signals Ary R.E. Sunday, 34 Runny to various (indecipherable)	

Army Form C. 2118.

WAR DIARY
or
INTELLIGENCE SUMMARY of 1st Col. 9th Manitoba Regt.
(Erase heading not required.)   2nd C.I.B. 1st Cdn. Inf. Bde.
October 1916.

(Instructions regarding War Diaries and Intelligence Summaries are contained in F. S. Regs., Part II. and the Staff Manual respectively. Title Pages will be prepared in manuscript.)

Place	Date	Hour	Summary of Events and Information	Remarks and references to Appendices
Rumencourt	23/10/16		Private Tittenton A.V.C. (T.F.) refused to be inoculated with Anti-Typhoid. He was a private Typhoid Carrier Serial No. 76. He has a conscientious objection to being inoculated. He was unwilling to receive this. He done. This was in about 4½ years of age & again 18 months as a reinforcement to the 1st A/South Wales. He has the full knowledge of the QMS of his Division that he was not seen in control thereof & Capt. ... Entitlement to see his Papers belonging to former Division are reported to Capt. Gill near Pol. (T.F.) the difficulties from Mange. The horses with not be used so far not as there. The Larry as Pathie murhes & of horses, and I have asked the attention of yet Col. French thinking to the fact that the horses are fit for short range. & Capt. Ferries horses are not fit to fair work or range. I. Ferrier says its do want to his but thrown improper treatment in the rear of officers actin not being noted by the Troops.	
	24/10/16		Very heavy all day. Inspected A Battery 23 Brig. in the Govern. The Horses are all looking well & in good condition. They are all under cover. The tent infected bag with teeth bright enough & & was utterly thrown into but roof of cover of cages. However sent A.V.S. of his feet [?]	
	25/10/16		Incantain as Above.	
	26/10/16		Visited Select. B. of Cav. B. at Bulliemont.	
			D. D. Rimerry 3rd Army inspected animal for remount returns at. A.V.S. He was the interest in an using moving to that later on throw down, D.D.V.S. 3rd Army also rattled A.A. of 11 Div. for A Div. for movement. Received [?] sending of [?] Major of Enq.	

2449 Wt. W14957/M90 750,000 1/16 J.B.C. & A. Form/C.2118/12.

Army Form C. 2118.

WAR DIARY
or
INTELLIGENCE SUMMARY

(Erase heading not required.)

of A.D. Army Corps
A.D.V.S. 46th (Nth Mid) Division
October 1916. 8th Sheet

Place	Date	Hour	Summary of Events and Information	Remarks and references to Appendices
BAVINCOURT	27/10/16		Weekly Conference of V.O.s	
	28/10/16		Major McLelland A.D.V.S. 39th Division came to tea & stays the night over my billet that of the 1/2 N. Mid. F.A.	
	29/10/16		On to Division in relieving us.	
	30/10/16		Went to DAS & saw ADVS 30th Division. Probably annual inspection emeuts at A.D.V.S. Inspected every the 515th (How.) Battery R.F.A. Had two just arrived from England. The 232nd Brigade. The horses are lightly "undetermined" condition. A few of them are very poor. Those are mostly old, fair old freddeders. The horses are well looked after but sittling more shelter in a muddy field day + to rainfall.	
	31/10/16.		Divl. No. 2. Academie. Divisional Headquarters moved to FROHEN-LE-GRAND. Left our Hay turn (fresh) behind at BEAURE PAIRE with 2/1th Brecon F.A.R. of to wait to be have to come any further.	

W.M.Bryall
Lt.Col.ng
A.D.V.S. 46th (Nth Mid) Division.

WAR DIARY of Lt Colonel Henry Drury D.S.O. 4th (North Midland) Division
R.F.A. 46th (North Midland) Division

Attached to War Diary for October 1916

WAR DIARY
or
INTELLIGENCE SUMMARY

Army Form C. 2118.

(Erase heading not required.)

Instructions regarding War Diaries and Intelligence Summaries are contained in F. S. Regs., Part II. and the Staff Manual respectively. Title Pages will be prepared in manuscript.

Place	Date	Hour	Summary of Events and Information	Remarks and references to Appendices

MANGE CHART. 46th DIVISION
PERIOD. MARCH 16th - OCT 31st 1916

B.A.C.

B. Sub/Bty, 232nd Brigade R.F.A.

WEEKLY PERIODS

WAR DIARY
INTELLIGENCE SUMMARY

Army Form C. 2118.

Vol 17

1st Cavalry (Indian) Brigade / H.Q 7th Indian Brigade / G.O.C. 4th Cav.(Ind) Division
November 1916.
1 - Sheet.

Place	Date	Hour	Summary of Events and Information	Remarks and references to Appendices
FROHEN-LE-GRAND	1/11/16		Went by motor to BEAUREPAIRE with Captain C. Hertz (?E) to see Buy Buy to see arrangements for lines moved up that to BOUQUEMAISON Station for evacuation to No.29 Stationary Hospital Abbeville	
	2/11/16		Divisional H.Q.'s moved from FROHEN-LE-GRAND to ST RIQUIER. H.Q. 1st Ind. Inf. Bde. also moved to ST RIQUIER.	
	3/11/16		Went by motor to No 29 Brit. Hospital & saw my two orderlies. Just arrived this morning. Saw Major Hopley also called on the Director of Medical Services. Visited H.Q.'s & Units of 137th Infantry Bde. with D.D.G.M.S.	
	4/11/16		" " " " 138th " " "	
	5/11/16		" " " " 139th " " "	
	6/11/16		The animals of all three Infantry Brigades are under cover with the exception of horses of the Record Regt. & the mules of 3rd Fly. reception of horses of Infantry. The Infantry animals have also the march field ambulances. A few pack animals though high up are fairly well sheltered but are not the regl. pack animals. High up General Henry Jenn carried out the suggest. I thought went I would give great care in few days and try to get the pack animals down. Yesterday tied there I saw of the fact that we were in draft also is wrong to be regard as full ground we had no cover except the ground.	

WAR DIARY
or
INTELLIGENCE SUMMARY

Army Form C. 2118.

Instructions regarding War Diaries and Intelligence Summaries are contained in F. S. Regs., Part II. and the Staff Manual respectively. Title Pages will be prepared in manuscript.

(Erase heading not required.)

of Lt. Colonel Macdougall

November 1916

2nd Sheet

Place	Date	Hour	Summary of Events and Information	Remarks and references to Appendices
St Riquier	6/11/16	Cont.	Inspected Signal Coy R.E. Lines which were low lying & swampy & had the animals removed. They have been put under cover in "lean to" sheds &c;	
	7/11/16		Very wet. Inspected animals of Field Coys R.E. with Captain T. Thomson AVC (T.F.) G.O.C postponed his inspection of these Units.	
	8/11/16		Inspected animals of 453rd Coy A.S.C. at Wrench. " " of No. 4 Section 46th D.A.C.	
	9/11/16		Attended the G.O.C's inspection of 452nd, 453rd, and 454th Coys A.S.C. I am proceeding on ten days leave of absence to England tomorrow. Captain E. Hartley AVC (T.F.) will act as A.D.V.S during my absence.	
	10/11/16		Proceeded on leave to England. Crossed same day. Left Boulogne at 1 P.M. arrived Folkstone 2.30 P.M. and London (Victoria) about 7 P.M.	
	19/11/16		Arrived Folkstone 6 P.M.	
	20/11/16		Left Boulogne by train at 10 A.M. and arrived at Div. H.Qrs at St Riquier about 3.30 P.M.	
	22/11/16		Went to No. 22 Base Veterinary Hospital to see my lame horse. Saw Major Hebday about him	
	23/11/16		Marched with Div. H.Qrs to FROHEN-LE-GRAND.	
	23/11/16		" " " " " LUCHEUX.	

WAR DIARY
INTELLIGENCE SUMMARY

of Lt Colonel M.M. M'Dougall
A.D.V.S. 46th (N.Midland) Division

November 1916

3 Sheet

Date	Hour	Summary of Events and Information	Remarks
27/11/16		Visited units billeted in HUMBERCOURT, WARLUZEL, and COUTURMONT. Inspected animals for evacuation at M.V.S. 6 animals evacuated of which 6 belonged to 46th Divn. + 10 from other formations.	
28/11/16		Visited units billeted in BREVILLE RS. and LE SOUICH.	
29/11/16		Inspected animals of 149th Bde R.F.A. (4 Batteries) and 150th Bde R.F.A. (3 Batteries) 46 to Divn. ½ A temporarily attached to 46 to Divn. "D" Bty. B Rty. A Bty. C Bty.(horses worn out). To order the tails to refer to the quarters of train animals in order to make the number of 150th belonging to the horse Batteries are much improving after tro bad trips they had for the Somme. Feet of U.V.S. Billeted generally being executed but laid not as clean as they said to Every (?). Never got very clean as they +- expected. 40 Animals were evacuated of which belonged to 46 to Divrs. + are believed to belong to yet Cavalry Divn. 38 belonged to the 30 Divn Artillery ½ of which is incapable debility. Ones - Bad conservt of them, according to Report of O.C. Mob. Vet. S.	

M.M. M'Dougall Lt Colonel
A.D.V.S. 46th (N.Midland) Divn.

WAR DIARY of A.D.V.S. Colonel Ummathought
INTELLIGENCE SUMMARY. A.D.V.S. 46th (N. Midland) Division

Army Form C. 2118.

1st Sheet — 18

Place	Date	Hour	Summary of Events and Information	Remarks and references to Appendices
LUCHEUX	1/12/16		Weekly Conference of O/s totalling A2ob of 46th Division/ stated with the 30th Division. Returns of 30th Divl Artillery included in the 46th Divl Artillery being due to Sig: St. Leger 4 sau: Sergeant Corbet A.V.C.(T.F.) attached to 2nd St. LEGER are under orders on p/qr 139th Infantry Bde. 5th and 6th Sherwood Foresters/ 4/4th N. Mid Field Ambulance. Three cases of "pricked up race" under treatment.	
	2/12/16		M.V.S. evacuated 8 animals belonging to Brimstone others from 46th Division try/ mly 30th Divl Artillery & 46th Canadian Divn. Was made to Wefech the sick animal/before evacuation Inspected animals for evacuation at D.V.S.	
	3/12/16		of 23rd Bde R.F.A. as they marched into LUCHEUX.	
	4/12/16		Went to see A.D.V.S. 49th (W.R.) Division at 4E.W.y and arranged with him that the 1/1st N. Mid N.V.S. and 1/11th W.Rg N.V.S. should more on morning of 6/12/16 taking over each others rides Also rode to the 1/1st N. Mid N.V.S. at ACRINCOURT with A A.D.S. 49th Divn.	
	5/12/16		Reports/ animals/ for evacuation at M.V.S.	
	6/12/16		Cpt C. Gentry A.V.C.(T.F.) Proceeded on ten days leave to England. Cpt T. Thompson A.V.C.(T.F.) who returned from leave on 4/12/16 took over command of 1/1st N. Mid N.V.S. during Cpt Gentry's absence. 1/1/1st N. Mid N.V.S. moved	

WAR DIARY of Lt. Col. S. Maurbruch, G.O.C. 46th (N. Mid.) Division

INTELLIGENCE SUMMARY

2nd Sheet

Place	Date	Hour	Summary of Events and Information	Remarks and references to Appendices
HENU	7/2/16		Divisional Headquarters moved to HENU. Inspected arrivals for evacuations at M.D.S.	
	8/2/16		Weekly conference of G.O.C.	
	9/2/16		Inspected lines of 1st Battery 2 & 2nd Bde R.F.A. at GRINCOURT where 48th (S. Midland) Division they had new left behind a reserve of "Limousins". They have been under instruction for sometime by 49th (W. Rdg) Division. Drive 54 cars are sent to refit under retrieved Rivers 30 and 60 lorries on all machines of this divisions are employed until D.O.S. 46th Div. for a supply of oil. I have arranged with D.O.S. 46th Div. to make a thorough inspection of the kinds. It was too bad today to inspect Limbers & Salcher wire have been to inland [illegible]. Supplies of Quickline & Salcher have been to inland for use. Continued the tour of the trenches, potches are being put in to bury or try the Clifting.	
	11/2/16		Inspected himself C.M.V.S. and saw 2 official cases of fever which had been received from 246th Bde R.F.A. & O.C. 49th (W. Rdg) Division. 246th Bde R.F.A. (1 Battery) = 2 cases 49th D.A.C. (Inf Sec) = 3 " (4 delivered cases) C/6/1 L Bentley my Groom — Awarded on 10 days leave to England. Inspected VIIth C.C.S. "Valois" today for April at L.E.G.20. 18 T.B.O.N. & worte to D.O.T.S. 3rd Army for arrival of certain things & parted in connection with it.	

WAR DIARY or INTELLIGENCE SUMMARY

Army Form C. 2118.

of H. Cloud Mencourt of G.O. 3rd & 4th Cav Regts
3rd Sheet

Place	Date	Hour	Summary of Events and Information	Remarks and references to Appendices
	12/12/16.		Inspected the Mange cases of 49th Div Artillery at 11th F.A./V.S. at 11 A.M. with Lt. Cloud A.W. Weir A.D.V.S. 49th Division. At 10 A.M. Lieut. "Eve Hospital" Geo Turner at Div H.Qrs. and went into the cases when this number — No 3 is my age. Visited Div. Field WARLINCOURT and GAUDIEMPRÉ. Inspected animals treated on Employ of Mange in line of 49 B. Battery 246. Field R.F.A. – Six belonging to B/246 Bttery had just been clipped were affected with mange & were to be sent to M.V.S. to receive the treatment.	
	13/12/16.		Inspected animals for exercise of M.V.S. – O.C. 1/1st F.Md./V.S. was unable to get the animals fed in the Hospital at WARLINCOURT owing to railway shelling in vicinity of that station. The R.T.O. directed him to take them to MONDICOURT where he succeeded in getting them entrained about 9 P.M.	
	14/12/16.		Weekly Conference of V.Os. Inspected horses of C.ay. 2 Bde R.F.A. 16th Division with D.D.V.S. 3rd Army. – 43 Cases noted under treatment. About 15 animals have got Harness Sores or skin eruptions the results of Harness, dirty to rest, it is going to the battery for clothing heads. Were issued earlier, battery today, from E.A.D.V.S.	
	15/12/16.			
	16/12/16.		Inspected transport animals & teams of 137th Infantry Regt. & was they of 4th Division Regt.	

1577 Wt. W10791/1773 500,000 1/15 D. D. & L. A.D.S.S./Forms/C. 2118.

WAR DIARY

INTELLIGENCE SUMMARY.

Army Form C. 2118.

St Alfred Murs Duff
a. D.M.S. 46th Midd Down
to Shief

Place	Date	Hour	Summary of Events and Information	Remarks and references to Appendices
HENU	17/12/16		Inspected arrivals for evacuation at M.D.S.	
	18/12/16		Went to 137th Infantry Bde to instruct Sergeant Dawson A.V.C.(T.F.) as to the clothing of the arrival, Facstup'd R.A on tree ADVS. go to Drocourt, the Division which is in use hearing 11th Corps Change. Paw the Captain E. Chattell R.V.C. (T.F.) R.C. and gave him as to duties.	
	19/12/16		Went round to the Q.A. Workings with Staff Captain of 46 Div. and gave instructions as to which could be dealt with by 46 Q.A. if forced into hospital as in reports which could not be evacuated by the 2 Bde R.F.A. are up in the firing line. The whole of the 46th Bde R.F.A. & 6th Bde R.F.A 49 to Div. were here themselves "horse hushed" + militated. The arrivals of + 3 Section 46 D.P. are due to go to the line until the late + Standing report by the carrying Section of + 9th Div. here were thoroughly dealt with.	
	20/12/16		For evacuation of M.D.S. Inspected the Forces of Aug 5 to Capt R.A. and no. of -3 Sectors O.A.C 13th (W. Rdg.) Division on 11 D.A.S. all stores were fitted with Range. The 49th Sect Artillery here today to moving of the ostron Division and the 46th D.A.O have left the 46 Division by 22nd instant.	
	21/12/16		Inspected Ration parts arrivals at Thurmgate and 13th D.A.O F. Morn. Reg. 132nd W. Rdg. Div. A.O. Gp. 6-9 Sprogs Form. G.T. & Ferand Fountain & St Laurent and 1/2 Field Ambulance.	

WAR DIARY
INTELLIGENCE SUMMARY.
(Erase heading not required.)

Army Form C. 2118.

The Colonel View Borrall
A.D.V.S.
5th Ind. 46th (N. Mid.) Division

Place	Date	Hour	Summary of Events and Information	Remarks and references to Appendices
HENU	21/2/16		Inspected Standings of No 3 Section R.A.O. which are being brought prior to reoccupation by the animals of No 3 Section 46th R.A.O. moving to ease of mange, having occurred in No 3 Section 49th D.A.C. which returns the Section yesterday. Inspected the horses of 1st & 2nd Sections, 49th Divl D.A.C. (3rd Section has been to Nauchin Park at HENU about 16 Tomos). One case (1st Section 2nd line Zille which will have to be executed) remains in an ambulance.	
	22/2/16		Weekly Inspection of No. 3. Inspected animals for evacuation at No 43. Inspected animals of C/242nd Regt R.F.A. 48th (So. Mid.) Division. 12 cases of Mange was still under treatment & the clipping is being delayed owing to want of clipping Suits. Major A. Lloyd Jones, D.S.O. D.A.D.V.S. 46th Division went over cases listed at FONQUEVILLERS, listed on Returns to 10.20 (D.A.V.S.)	
	23/2/16		Inspected Units of D.A.C. & animals of No 2 Section. (Attended Major Lloyd Jones funeral in afternoon)	
	24/2/16		Inspected animals of 4th & 5th Sections.	
	25/2/16		Inspected Units of 1/2nd to Bys R.F.A. to Sats of which are being disinfected. The slow housing of No 4.5th was stopped during the afternoon of the day owing to the arrival of mange in a drip of 3rd Btn for the Lambs. Saft Captain Larmour in charge of 40 horses of Horse in the afternoon.	
	26/2/16		D.V.S. 3rd Army cycled at my Office & went to HRTD in tone lines of D.A.C. - 2 3rd Bye R.F.A. and 1/3 2nd Section Bys to R.F.A. Also N.V.S.	

WAR DIARY
INTELLIGENCE SUMMARY

Army Form C. 2118.

Instructions regarding War Diaries and Intelligence Summaries are contained in F.S. Regs., Part II. and the Staff Manual respectively. Title pages will be prepared in manuscript.

(Erase heading not required.)

Place	Date	Hour	Summary of Events and Information	Remarks and references to Appendices
HENU	27/12/16		Lectured on "Horse & Stable Management" at GAUDIEMPRE at 2.30 P.M. The Lecture was for Young & inexperienced Officers. Only about 13 Officers attended & about 18 N.C.O's. All Transport Officers of 137th Infantry Bgde. were present & only 2 R.A. officers from Bde. The Young Officers for whom the Lecture was principally intended were absent.	
	28/12/16		Inspected animals for evacuation at M.V.S. Inspected States of 230th Bgde R.F.A. which had been "Oto-lauded" & otherwise disinfected. The horses were allowed to go into their lines today.	
	29/12/16		Usually conference of 2 P.M. Inspected animals returned by 137th to 118 Bgy. Staff of "N" Staff.	
	30/12/16		A. B. & D. Batteries 282 Bde R.F.A. to find out what horse clipping machines were in charge & what had their indents for to;	
	31/12/16		Inspected animals for evacuation at M.V.S.	

N.W. Brigade
A.D.V.S. 46th (N. Mid.) Division.

of Lt. Colonel N.W. Brigade
A.D.V.S. 46th (N. Mid.) Division
O-Sheet

N.W. Brigade
Lt. Colonel
A.D.V.S. 46th (N. Mid.) Division.

WAR DIARY
of Lt. Colonel Macdonagh, A.D.M.S. 46th (N. Mid) Division.

INTELLIGENCE SUMMARY. January 1917. 1st page.

Vol 19. Army Form C. 2118.

Place	Date	Hour	Summary of Events and Information	Remarks and references to Appendices
HENU	3rd Jany		Lectured on Rheumatism at Q/2nd Essex R.F.A. at 2.30 P.M.	
	4th "		Inspected the lines of 6/2nd Bde R.F.A. at GRINCOURT. Fine cold & dry — men well put-up-&-clad. Reviewed all right, looking well. Visited to help.	
	5th "		Weekly Conference of M.Os. Inspected arrivals for evacuation at M.V.S. Conf. Parades my greatest effort to LEROY FARM, PREVENT (annual) — Reviewed my greatest effort to bring my Bay Horse (bright) — there was very returned to Duo frore F.2.Q Conf the hospital — where he had been operated on for "Buttor" N.F. He recovered. Looking fit and Sound.	
	6th "		Inspected arrivals of 4 to 45th Division at St Amand, in the memory of those of 4 to 5th Leicesters. 188th F.A., 1/2nd Field Coy R.E. at Caudescure in the afternoon.	
	7th "		Sunday in Office.	
	8th "		General Sir Edmund Allenby K.C.B. Commanding Third Army, &c.F. devoted the riffles of operating territorial officers and others ranks of the 46th Division in the New Year's Honours at HENU at 10 A.M. today. I attended to parade and received Inspected to do recruiting upon treatment in G/2nd Bde R.F.A., in also inspected arrivals for evacuation at M.V.S.	

WAR DIARY or INTELLIGENCE SUMMARY

Army Form C. 2118.

W. H. Horwill / Marlborough
38/13 46th (NM) Division
January 1917   Page 2.

Place	Date	Hour	Summary of Events and Information	Remarks and references to Appendices
HENU	9th January		Dipping Bath to see how the repairs were progressing in afternoon.	
	10- "		Lectured in Cinema Hut at St Amand at 2.30 P.M. on First Aid Nursing &c of Bed Cases.	
	11- "		Inspected animals & lines of 1/2 N. Md. Field Ambulance.	
	12- "		Weekly Conference of T.M.Os. Inspected Manuals for evacuation at M.V.S. in afternoon.	
	13- "		Inspected 6th D. Staffs & 6th S. Staffs & inspected Transport animals & horse lines.	
	14- "		Inspected certain cases at M.V.S. with officer i/c M.V.S.	
	15- "		Visited 1/4 & 1/5 Gy ASC inspecting Clearing & Disposing Machines.	
	16- "		Inspected animals for Evacuation at M.V.S. in afternoon. Inspected animals & lines of L.O.3 Sector 2/1st Reserve Park in morning.	Kevin & Irving & Pankhurst front
	17- "		Lectured at St Amand at 4.30 P.M. in Cinema Hall, this completed the series of Lectures ordered in D.R.O. 2377 dated 25/12/16. The subjects dealt with: — (1) Horse & Field Management (2) First aid Treatment (3) The ordinary forms of Wastage, Horse sickness & injuries their prevention & treatment. Four lectures were given; 1 at M.V.S., 3 at St Amand.	

WAR DIARY
INTELLIGENCE SUMMARY

Army Form C. 2118.

Lt. Colonel W.H.W. Bryant
A.D.M.S. 46th (N.Mid) Division

January 1917   Page 3

Place	Date	Hour	Summary of Events and Information	Remarks and references to Appendices
HÉNU	18 Jany		Inspected A, B, C & D Cottage, 231st Bde R.F.A. in their lines at P.A.S. — Snow & frost.	Freezing hard over 20 degrees of frost at night.
	19 "		Weekly conference of M.Os. Captain C.V. Rogers of A.V.C. (T.C.) T.O. i/c VIIth Corps Heavy Artillery called to see me about a general matter regarding training of R.O.C. VIIth Corps N.A. — Sent copy eventually to D.D.M.S. 3rd Army on the subject. Snow & frost.	
	20 "		Inspected further Billets & one at M.F.C. in afternoon	
	21 "		Inspected the lines of No. 451st, 453rd, 454th Coys A.S.C. 453rd Coy Lines were satisfactory. The lines & lines of 451st and 454th Coys require considerable improvement especially the 451st Coy. The snow into which they had been carried off to a considerable extent if 453rd Coy, but very has been done to the other Companies. As the lines of 462nd Coy Vermont & their lines were not been visited.	
	"		Inspected arrivals for evacuating D.I.S	
	"		Selection A 46 & B & C	
	22 "		Arrived at 1st E. Mid Field Ambulance	
	23 "		" called off Prev Offrs about 12.30 P.M.	
	24 "		Inspected arrivals for evacuating at M.V.S.	
	25 "		Weekly Conference of M.Os. Inspected C/232 2nd Bgde R.F.A. in afternoon	
	26 "		Inspected three I/O & Lewis Mess which he? they attend of 46th Div	
	27 "		Signal/? Office hunt the day. Sent one to M.V.S. for Supplies? temp	
			D.D.M.S 3rd Army called at?	

WAR DIARY
INTELLIGENCE SUMMARY

Army Form C. 2118.

Lt Colonel McCorquodale
A.D.V.S. 46th (N. Mid) Division
Page 4

January 1917

Place	Date	Hour	Summary of Events and Information	Remarks and references to Appendices
AENU	27th		Inspected Horses of 4.5.3rd — Coy A.S.C. +C.	Snowing & intense frost. Roads very slippery.
	28th		Inspected Revl. N.Z. Farms. Clipping had carried out at 09:00 A.M.	
			Captain Shaw Buttons sent his Chevaul Under Army to M.V.S.	
	29th		Inspected No 2 Section R.A.C. in afternoon.	
	30th		Inspected 10 Horses of South Mids. which are attached to M.V.S. 46. Divn., they were in fairly good condition, several free from skin injuries.	
			Inspected 1, 2nd S. Mid. ½ Coy R.E. — The animals have been in the open for over a fortnight & a considerable number are very "tucked up" — Arranges therefore with RME to build stables for these horses. Also inspects animals of 2/1st S. Mid. ½ Coy RE in the same state. They are in good condition, & are those of 2nd/3rd S. Mid. ½ Amberland which are also expected could if the animals of Cs.33 — Bgd. R.F.A. which have improved in condition. They are not fretting on flat ground to have to toe clipping. Gave a few tips to protect of C/W. Smith Cumberl stating that & had examined a horse reported by him as being likely to prove useful for breeding & was of the opinion the animal was not likely to prove useful for breeding purposes — This Vety Certificate was required before he could sell off	
	31st		Inspected Horses of A.B.C. +D Batteries 2 Bn 7th Bgds. R.F.A. in their Lines & also inspected a few sick cases at M.V.S.	

W M Bruce Lt Colonel
A.D.V.S. 46th North Midland Division
B.E.F.

1/2/17

WAR DIARY
INTELLIGENCE SUMMARY

Army Form C. 2118.

Lt. Colonel Walter Powell D.D.O.
A.D. & S. 46th (Nth) Divisions

Hard frost.

VM 20

Place	Date	Hour	Summary of Events and Information	Remarks and references to Appendices
HENU	1st Feb		Inspected tartness of 2/2nd 3rd Bgde RFA with Captain G. Hartley AVC & D who is in temporary Veterinary charge of this Brigade during the absence of Captain G.A.Glass AVC(TF). Sent four (4) horses to MVS for Inspected mange and isolated 14 others.	
"	2nd "		Weekly Conference of VO's. Visit to Coulomby in afternoon regarding 188th Co. & 3rd Quarters Staff facility put under cover.	
"	3rd "		Inspected horses of 2/232nd AFA 2/C Armed with Capt. Hartley. They are looking well & the clipping is being pushed on.	
"	4th "		Some clipping that is +ve to +ve returns, refused by D.A.D.O.S. & two milk spinning team were supplied.	
"	5th "		Returns today for horses issued to D/235 to 239 RFA = 4 top stallions
			2/235 to 239 RFA = 1 completed & 8 top + billion-hito	
			" = 3 top stallions	
"	6th "		457 Coy A.S.C. returned to D.A.O.S. Would not cut and had to be informed to D.A.O.S. Inspected animals of 2/232nd Bgde Brig Field Artillery with DADS vm. A.B.C. and D Batteries & B/A.C.L.C. Battery Ounds before the attends of Horsetan Batteries, & the B.A.C. appearing improvement. The supply of clipping was very great exhausted & there was not sufficient for them. So clipping is about coming to a standstill. Industry drawings & troughs for 7 & 54 Coys ASC Working slightly. Two 457 & 454 Coys ASC	

WAR DIARY
or
INTELLIGENCE SUMMARY.

Army Form C. 2118.

Lt Colonel MacDougall
A.D.V.S. 46th Division
Page 2

Place	Date	Hour	Summary of Events and Information	Remarks and references to Appendices
HENU	8th Feby		Inspected 46th DAC (Echelon A) & BAC 232nd Bde RFA	Hard frost.
"	9th		Weekly Conference of V.O's.	
"	10th		Sy Office. Weekly returns &c.	
"	11th		Inspected 232 to Bde RFA with the exception of "B" Battery	
"	12th		Slight tendency to thaw	
"	13th		Thawing gradually	
"	14th		Strong N-E during night & wind & snow storm setting in	
			Inspected animals for evacuation to DVS	
"	16th		Weekly Conference of V.O's	
"	17th		Inspected animals V.S. Leicester Regt, 6th & 7th Staffs Regt, 186 & 11 Coy and C/232 Bde Army F.A.	
"	18th		Proceeded to leave to England. Capt. C. Hartley A.V.C (T.F) takes over (have reported for duty with 232 Bde AFA G.O.C & S.) during my absence. Lt O'Brien with reference to the	
"	19th		Inspected stable of Govt Infantry stable at Gouy-en-Artois with reference to the disinfection. Reported adversely. Ch	
"	20th		46th D.H.Q. moves to Gouy-en-Artois. Office in Nissen Hut in Orchard. Steady rain all day. Ch.	
GOUY EN ARTOIS.	21st		Inspected animals for Evacuation at Hd N.M.V.S, Stocked office of A.D.V.S 6th Div. and inspected some animals of # 81 # 84 Bty, A.P.C with Capt FACER CA	

Army Form C. 2118.

WAR DIARY
or
INTELLIGENCE SUMMARY.
(Erase heading not required.)

Instructions regarding War Diaries and Intelligence Summaries are contained in F. S. Regs., Part II. and the Staff Manual respectively. Title pages will be prepared in manuscript.

Place	Date	Hour	Summary of Events and Information	Remarks and references to Appendices
GOUY-EN-ARTOIS.	22/2/17		Rested transport of #66 & #68 Fd Coys R.E. & 1st Monmouths at SIMENCOURT. Horses in open and on very bad ground.	
	23/2/17		Met V.Os at billet of 1/1st M.M.V.S. ERINCOURT.	

C. Hartley
Captain A.V.C.
for Lt Col A.D.V.S. 46th Division.

Army Form C. 2118.

WAR DIARY
or
INTELLIGENCE SUMMARY

of Lt. Colonel Wemyss Bryant
A.D.V.S. 46th (N. Mid.) Division.

(Erase heading not required.)

Vol. I Page 1. Page 2.

Instructions regarding War Diaries and Intelligence Summaries are contained in F. S. Regs., Part II. and the Staff Manual respectively. Title Pages will be prepared in manuscript.

Place	Date	Hour	Summary of Events and Information	Remarks and references to Appendices
HENU.	1/3/17		D.H.Q. returns to HENU.	
	2/3/17		Weekly conference of V.O's. Inspected some horses of 4/5 & 4/5 Bgde A.C. CH	
	3/3/17		Visited wagon lines of 231 Bgde R.F.A., C4.	
	4/3/17		Inspected remounts at SAULCOURT. Moderate many of them showing signs of recent skin diseases (C.H.)	
	5/3/17		Lt. Colonel Wemyss Bryant A.D.V.S. 46th (N. Mid.) Division rejoins from leave about 12. P.M.	
	6/3/17		Capt. C. Hartley, A.V.C. (T.F.) returned to command 1/1 N. Mid. M.V.S. from Divl. H.Q. who asked to had been acting as A.D.V.S. during absence of Lt. Colonel Wemyss Bryant. Inspected animals for evacuation at M.V.S.	
	7/6/17			
	8/3/17		Inspected animals of H.Q. section D.A.C. & was struck at the percentage on a kind suffering from extreme debility. Many suffering of Stomach Complaint, also from a throwing condition, also critical condition probably due to resting due to short of grit. Inspected A. & D. Batteries 230 - Bgde R.F.A.	

Army Form C. 2118.

WAR DIARY
or
INTELLIGENCE SUMMARY
(Erase heading not required.)

Lt. Colonel Harris Russell
B.D.V.S. 46 (N. Mid.) Division.

Page 2.

Place	Date	Hour	Summary of Events and Information	Remarks and references to Appendices
HENU	9th March		Conference of V.O's of my office. Colonel N.W. Kuria- Congratulated B.S.O. D.D.V.S. 5th Army called at my office also Lt. Colonel Shelly D.D.V.S. 5th Army. Attended Conference of officers at D.D.V.S. 6th Army HQrs at RAINCHEVAL. The 46th (N.Mid.) Division was transferred to V th Corps V to Army from 12 noon on 9/3/17.	
	10th "		Inspected two Horses (Riders) at H.S. which were received in a state of exhaustion on evening of 9 inst. Two horses were debilitated & unfit for race. Visited Brig General right standing tour, was furnished to Brig HQrs. They have been shackled in route & should, probably, be the South Pink. Horses(?) we collected 61st & 62nd & I Sec of 46th Bgr at DOULLENS on 9th inst. & brought them to D.A.C. where they were handed over to VII Corps of D.A.C. D.46. D.A.C. The Aitia horses of 282 By A Bring ?A ?A ?Lieut O'Brien A.V.C. wished not 11 horses which are in for M.V.S. on Tuesday 13 inst. Inspected Horses of 260 with Kin & with Captain Tremley H.O. 230 Bgr 13 FOTRS Inspected Horses of 454 ?A & 454 ?Gps C.26 with Capt Brauntons H.V.C.(T) These are light in condition and are being worked hard. Inspected animals of 1/1 N.Mid. Field Amp Blanco, & 1 Bg H.Q. Coy in afternoon.	
	11th "			
	12th "			
	13th "		Supervised tables 29(?) of Brigade Rtg for life of March. They are elaborating after first day, but improve early up til 9 pm.	

Army Form C. 2118.

WAR DIARY
or
INTELLIGENCE SUMMARY Royal Warwickshire
(Erase heading not required.) 2/6 & 1/6 Batt Warwick Division

Page 3.

Place	Date	Hour	Summary of Events and Information	Remarks and references to Appendices
HENU	14th March		Rode to BAYENCOURT – SAILLY-AU-BOIS and HÉBUTERNE with the object of seeing the nature of the ground over which the Artillery ammunition is to go to HÉBUTERNE. As it was 5 P.M. when I got to HÉBUTERNE it was too late to proceed beyond that place. The route from SAILLY-AU-BOIS to HÉBUTERNE are very bad & was going, met Captain T. Thomson A.V.C.(T) who recommended that use that the ford HÉBUTERNE & states that there is the ground to avoid running through the village of HÉBUTERNE. My next thought is to avoid the road from SAILLY-AU-BOIS. Bad in daylight & very bad in the dark. Many traps exist to	
	15th		inflict men & animals for evacuation at M.V.S. mostly "Rabbit" cases from the Artillery. The times of the Arrival of R.A. are being very much decreased in getting up Ammunition to the Guns or keeping the Guns going, and the Ammunition Transport being infrequent through very heavy going, while inspecting the Stretchers men returning from Tanques 7th & 8th...	
	16th		...each infantry Battalion as to their fitness for inspection... disinfect any Infestation...	
	17th		... Arranged with Captain L... Sent to 1st & 3rd field Ambulances for... 5/6, 6/2 – R.D.C. 1st and 2nd... field Ambulances 460, 468... 466 – D.D.C. 5th...	
	18th		... Chateau de la Haie... augment Hospital... Rode to Brigade Hd. Qts... A.B.and D. Batteries 2.8.1...	

Army Form C. 2118.

WAR DIARY
or
INTELLIGENCE SUMMARY of Lt Col J McDougall
A.D.V.S. 46th (Mid) Division
(Erase heading not required.)

Page 4

Place	Date	Hour	Summary of Events and Information	Remarks and references to Appendices
HÉNU	19th March		Went to COUIN. COIGNEUX - BAYENCOURT. CHATEAU-de-la-HAIE & SOUASTRE.	
"	20th "		Went to COUIN - & then to AUTHIE with Capt Clements to see the billets which had been occupied by MVS of 21st Division.	
			Inspected Animals for evacuation at MVS.	
COUIN	21st "		Bulk of Hd Qrs moved to COUIN	
"	22nd "		Inspected A & B Batteries 231st Bde Horses are all light and do aging & hard work. About 10 rather debilitated horses in "B" about half first number in "A".	
"	23rd "		Weekly Conference of VOs. Inspected 63 Animals for evacuation at MVS. chiefly Debility. Thy say "Lord Roberts" to being evacuated Tomorrow to N° 22 Vety Hospl.	
"	24th "		Went Visbar Thursday with regard to new Divisional Headquarters of COUIN and marched to VILLERS BOCAGE	
"	26th "		" VILLERS BOCAGE and marched to DURY	
"	28th "		" entrained at SALEUX and left there at 9.20 PM	
"	29th "		" arrived at LITTERS about 3 PM. Buck the D.D.V.S. (about 8.P Martin)	
NORRENT FONTES	30th "		NORRENT FONTES about 5 PM - Buck D.D.R. (Lionel Ryder) in the Village about 6 P.M. Found My Office for HdQrs had arrived leaving Couin.	

Army Form C. 2118.

WAR DIARY
or
INTELLIGENCE SUMMARY Lt. Colonel Graves Dowell
(Erase heading not required.) A.D.V.S. and O.C. M Dwmiers

Instructions regarding War Diaries and Intelligence Summaries are contained in F. S. Regs., Part II. and the Staff Manual respectively. Title Pages will be prepared in manuscript.

Place	Date	Hour	Summary of Events and Information	Remarks and references to Appendices
NORRENT FONTES	30th March		The A.T. Cols Sections joined the 46th Divl Signal Coy R.E. at Viliers Brewy on 25/3/17 and the animals were first seen by me at Dury on morning of 29/3/17 when I found practically all of them to be affected with Mange.	Page 5

Showed cases = 3
Marked cases = 9
Suspected " = 9
Apparently not affected but at any rate contacts = 3
Total 24

(1) Wired to D.A.V.S. Fifth Army on 29/3/17. "The horses of A.T. Cols Sections which have just joined the 46th Divn have affected with mange AAA twelve (12) marked cases probably scabies AAA nine (9) suspected AAA running three (3) animals shew no marked symptoms AAA recommend the evacuation of all the horses AAA A.D.V.S. 46th Division."

(2) To D.A.V.S. Fifth Army — V.M.3 - 28th March. "The horses of A.T. Cols Sections with harness and three pugs are being left at Dury by order of Fifth Army AAA one W.C.O. and twelve men left in charge AAA returned up to and incl. Aug 29th instant AAA Will you please arrange for above and reevacuation AAA the condition of the horses of stated herewith was reported to you yesterday by wire AAA A.D.V.S. 46th Division.

Army Form C. 2118.

WAR DIARY
or
INTELLIGENCE SUMMARY
(Erase heading not required.)

(A. Coy/ MG Bn.DvcH.
A.D.V.S. 4th Div Divncers.)

Page 6.

Place	Date	Hour	Summary of Events and Information	Remarks and references to Appendices
		(3)	To A.D.V.S. 46th Div.— V995—28th March. Am informed you are not in 5th Army but recommend evacuators of mange cases at first opportunity AAA would like to know number of A.T. Cold Shelters and where it came from AAA. A.D.V.S. 5th Army. (N.B.— This wire was evidently duplicated by D.D.V.S. before my arrival ~ wire was received by him.)	
		(4)	To D.D.V.S. Fifth Army.— VM4.—28th March. V935— AAA tried you today that all horses of A.T. Coys Shelters namely 24 were being left at Dury returned to 19th AAA only the vehicles are being filled and have been disinfected AAA refuse of which to A.T. Cold Shelter and came from 2nd Corps Signal Coy at BOUZINCOURT AAA the horses are left by the order of the Fifth Army AAA please arrange for evacuation AAA ALO V.S. 46th Div. Suspected animals of 148th Machine Gun Coy— This Unit now belongs to the 46th Divsn (Bgd—Dorsely) & has just come out from EngBhd. Strength 40 old mules & 4 riding horses. The animals are in good condition & are of good type.	
Norrent Fontes	31st March		Visited QUERNES, WITTERNESSE, BOMBY & MAZINGHEM with Staff Captain R.A. with the object of finding out if Quarters can be found in any of these places when the unit reaches it the following. Six Mule Teams shot at QUERNES today the unit, buried ...	

Army Form C. 2118.

WAR DIARY
or
INTELLIGENCE SUMMARY of Lt-Colonel W. McDougall
A.D.V.S. 46th (Nth Midland) Division
(Erase heading not required.)

Page 7.

Place	Date	Hour	Summary of Events and Information	Remarks and references to Appendices
NORRENT FONTES	31st March		No cases occurred in any of the other villages. Animals are said to have been destroyed at 81/598 and ROQUETOIRE both of which places are outside my area, & not going to be reoccupied by this Division. D.D.V.S. 1st Army confirmed the information regarding QUERNES being the only village in which cases of Glanders had occurred amongst animals of the Portuguese Army.	
"				

Headquarters
46th Division

W. McDougall
Lt-Colonel
A.D.V.S. 46th (North Midland) Division
B.E.F.

Forwarded
W. McDougall
Lt-Colonel
A.D.V.S. 46th (N.Md.) Division

Army Form C. 2118.

WAR DIARY
INTELLIGENCE SUMMARY
(Erase heading not required.)

Instructions regarding War Diaries and Intelligence Summaries are contained in F. S. Regs., Part II. and the Staff Manual respectively. Title Pages will be prepared in manuscript.

Col. Col. Wm Briggs C.B. C.V.O.
A.D.V.S. 46th (Nth) Div.

April 1917   Vol 2

Place	Date	Hour	Summary of Events and Information	Remarks and references to Appendices
NORRENT FONTES	1st April		Attended Conference of A.D.V.S.'s at Office of D.D.V.S. 1st Army, LILLERS.	
"	2nd "		1st F. Lt. M.V.S. arrived at FONTES. Visited 230th Bde R.F.A. at QUERNES, but it was snowing & too wet to see the horses.	
"	3rd "		Inspected animals for evacuation at M.V.S. Inspected horses of Divl Train :- 461st Coy = Poor (commented on for debility) 462 " = Fairly good 453 " = " " (Evacuated 2 debility & Mange) 454 " = Fairly good (Recommended that Divl Train should have field forage ration) Inspected most of the horses of 231st Bde R.F.A. A.T.D. Batteries found light & poor in condition, must at once put B & C Batteries taking weaker horses.	
"	4th to 7th "		Inspected animals of 8th Shewood For. to Col. Rely - in very good condition.	
"	8th "		Inspected animals of 2/3d Bde R.F.A. - Sent 10 to M.V.S. for casualties. A Battery = light & weak better but improving (Major Wood) B " " " " " " " (Major David) C " " = About ¾ in poor condition, rest good D " " = Twenty debilitated about ¼ Light horse (Major Wright) Inspected horses at M.V.S. in all 52 debility cases, 1 & 4 mange.	

Army Form C. 2118.

To Lt Colonel W. MacDougall A.D.S.
A.D.V.S. 46th (N. Mid) Division
Page 2

WAR DIARY
INTELLIGENCE SUMMARY
(Erase heading not required.)

Instructions regarding War Diaries and Intelligence Summaries are contained in F. S. Regs., Part II. and the Staff Manual respectively. Title Pages will be prepared in manuscript.

Place	Date	Hour	Summary of Events and Information	Remarks and references to Appendices
NORRENT FONTES	6th April		Weekly Conference of V.Os. Meet for Wks & inspected animals of following units:- 4th Leicester, 138th M.G Coy, 468th Field Coy R.E, 5th Leicesters, 1st Monmouths, 2nd N.Mid. Field Ambulance. Capt F. Druitsnuit A.V.C. (T.F.) accompanied me.	
"	7th "		Inspected animals of 4/6th Nor'l Cavalry R.E. " 6th Sherwood Foresters. In very good condition & looking well.	
"	"			
"	8th "		Moved H.Q. Inspected animals of 1 N.Mid. Field Ambulance. They are not looking very well & are short of Warbags, chone rags & cheynots (Easter Sunday). Conference of M.Os. to arrange for Lectures on Horsemastership to R.A and R.E White.	
"	9th "		Divisional March of all units of the Division into the exception of the Divl. Trains and M.V.S. Inspected the animals turning fitty 40, at they passed. Required a report to Divl R.Q. for information of I.A.C.	
"	11th "		Inspected animals for evacuation at M.V.S. about 24 animals of which 7 were large or Suspected Mange.	
"	12th "		Inspected animals of Mobiles 4/46th Bat.	
"	"		3/46th Bde	
"	"		" for evacuation at M.V.S.	
BUSNES	13th "		Divl. Headquarters moved to BUSNES. Also M.V.S. trains place.	

2449 Wt. W14957/M90 750,000 1/16 J.B.C. & A. Forms/C.2118/12.

Army Form C. 2118.

WAR DIARY
or
INTELLIGENCE SUMMARY
(Erase heading not required.)

Lt. Colonel Van Straubenzee A.D.C.
A.D. of S. 46th (N. Mid.) Division

April 1917

Page 3.

Place	Date	Hour	Summary of Events and Information	Remarks and references to Appendices
BUSNES	14th April		Weekly Conference of V.O.s	
"	15th "		Sunday - Inspected cases of Mange at N.V.S. from 457th Coy A.S.C.	
"	16th "		Inspected all the animals of 457th Coy A.S.C. for skin diseases and picked out 24 animals which were either affected or showing suspicious signs of Mange. They too all been dressed with Calcium Sulphide (ascertaining 7½ % of Sulphur) N.V.C. (T.F.) V.O. 45 & 46th M.V. (Brig.) & O. of 457 Coy & Senior V.O. Veterinary Dept. who did not consent of my going through these animals agree this morning as inspected as possible that animals were injected to go to Aubilland for Friesians burning. They are to be inspected & to be turned out. O.C. Brew & V.O. of V.O. of 457 Coy were present at inspection.
LABEUVRIERE.	17th "		Div. H. Qrs moved to Labeuvriere also Div. Signal Coy & 178th M.G. Coy. Atterberg & M.V.S. remained in BUSNES area.	
"	18 to "		Went over to O.C. Div. Train to 453rd - 451st & 454th Coys A.S.C. regarding Mange - Sent 5 horses to N.V.S. for Mange, viz: 453rd Coy = 2 & 454th Coy = 1, 457th Coy = 2, Total = 5	
"	19th "		Inspected the horses of 457th Coy A.S.C. which were picked out on 16th/4/17. Sent 1 horse to N.V.S. for mange. 8 N.C.O. I fund was also ruled with the Divisional officer. One of the 7 was a mare whose withers but for these.

2449   Wt. W14957/M90 750,000 1/16 J.B.C. & A. Forms/C.2118/12

WAR DIARY
INTELLIGENCE SUMMARY

Army Form C. 2118.

of 1st Batln Cameron Highrs 8 CSB
GOOS 246th (HLI) Division

1914

Place	Date	Hour	Summary of Events and Information	Remarks and references to Appendices
SAINS-EN-GOHELLE	20th April		Bn H. Qrs moved to SAINS-EN-GOHELLE. Saw H. Cloud & Nightingale en route to its rest centres as far as NOEUX-LES-MINES.	
"	21st "		Weekly Conference of V.O's	
"	22nd "		Rode to BARLIN and saw Captains Clegg A.&C. (3rd Canadian Division) commanding the Railhead N.S. about the three O.P.'s at BARLIN with a view to getting the names of the Bn. Int. Dept. put through the Bn.	
"	"		One distributed 18 names to Div. Signal Coy R.E. by 452nd, 453rd, & 454th Corps A.S.C. at BRAQUEMONT. The	
"	23rd "		Nonnes have improved in as Stores, but many of them repairs were greening especially in 452nd + 453rd Coys.	
"	"		This village is being shelled intermittently too or three minutes (6 P.M.)	
"	"		The front aspect of those was blown up by a shell about 3·30 P.M. and several horses in the main Street were hit during the day. It was turned to fires to in the evening.	
"	24th "		Inspected H.Q. + N.N. M.S. billet at K.18.B.36 (Sheet 36 C. Lens). Visited Horse Bathing Estabt at BARLIN with Capt. G. Lentz O.C (?) to see that the latter was being prepared for taking in Calvary horses.	
"	25th "		7·35 Animals were put through the Bath today from the following Units. Det. These 18th M.G. Coy; 4 few rifles of 1/37th Infantry Bde 138th M.G. Coy + a few rifles of 18th Infantry Bde; 1/1st R. Berks R.T.S & 1 Section of No 3 Sig Coy R.E.	

WAR DIARY / INTELLIGENCE SUMMARY

Army Form C. 2118.

(Erase heading not required.)

of Lt Col Menzies Croll O.A.O.
2.D.F.S. 46th (Nth) Division
Page 5.

Place	Date	Hour	Summary of Events and Information	Remarks and references to Appendices
SAINS-EN-GOHELLE	26th April		Went to BARLIN to see the dipping which was going on of animals of the Division. Animals dipped on 25th and 26th April.	

Unit — Number of Animals

46th Divnl Train
- 451st Coy A.S.C. — 108
- 452nd " " — 72
- 453rd " " — 96
- 454th " " — 40
  — 346

137th Infantry Brigade
- 137th Machine Gun Coy — 46
- 5th S. Staffs — 3
- 6th S. Staffs — 4
  — 53

138th Infantry Brigade
- 138th Machine Gun Coy — 40
- 5th Leicesters — 20
- 4th Lincolns — 18
- 5th Lincolns — 2
  — 17
  — 104

V.O. Superintending
Cpt. T. Whitworth 2nd L. (T.F.)
" " "
" " "
" " "
" " "
" " "
" " "

WAR DIARY
INTELLIGENCE SUMMARY

Army Form C. 2118.

H.Q. Colonel Manager ADVS 46th (Field) Division
a DAS. 46 (Field) Division

Place	Date	Hour	Summary of Events and Information	Remarks and references to Appendices
SAINS-EN-GOHELLE	April 26th		Visit to HQrs 46th Div. Signal Coy Number of Animals 26	No Superintending RVS
"			1st N. Md. Field Ambulance 50	Capt. + Lieutenants
"			3rd " " " 30	" "
"			2nd " " " 47	" "
"			4th " " " 104	" "
"			Sub Total = 610 Animals in the two days	
"			231st Bgde R.F.A. = 119 Animals, and 466th Field Coy R.E. = 54 animals	Plus C. Battery Captain R.F.A. M.O. Thomson Superintended
"			Grand Total 486 616 119 57	
"	24th		Weekly Conference of V.O.s at my Office	
"			Inspected 18 A.C. 28 Bgd Army F.A. Brigade at SAINS-EN-GOHELLE. Hay was well groomed, the equipment received good. The muster on the whole satisfactory for this Brigade. Although horses were a bit light	
"	28th		Visited trek, am. see half on the Island 1st Cycle Army Field Artillery numbers of 68th and 28th Battalions 14 Cycle Army Field Artillery. 68th Battery - fair to good condition. 23 Their Inv. or "Phor Lix" off more or less. They had been driven to the battlefield & now driven to rest area	

WAR DIARY or INTELLIGENCE SUMMARY

Army Form C. 2118.

Place	Date	Hour	Summary of Events and Information	Remarks and references to Appendices
SAINS EN GOHELLE	28th April Contd		14th Bgde Army Field Artillery (Contd)	
			88th Battery (rest of the horses are in very poor condition. The cause is in a trip by Travers on account of train for shelter & also their being the shellings old & wagons, & it is difficult now to say if the Horse will inhale oil & legions, & it is difficult now to say if the horse will ever recover from the effect of the train has cases of slaughter are not, but most of them bear of the trains were only those of "sudden".	
			Ord to Coy SERVING in afternoon. Five tee 104. Field Gy R.G. but was unable to find the unit.	
			Captain T Thornton A.V.C. (T.F.) is today superintending the Applying of the animals of A, B, C and D Batteries 2 Bde R.F.A. and B Battery 26 L.H. Bgde R.F.A.	
	29th		At BARLIN. Inspected animals of 289th Bgde Army F.A.	
			A Battery = Condition fairly fair throughout. Horses seem to be beginning to improve. (28 horses below establishment).	
			B Battery = Many of the animals are in quite good condition. This Battery should soon be alright.	
			C Battery = Fairly good, seem to be improving. (42 animals below establishment)	
			D Battery = Condition quite good about the pace, poor, but improving. (33 animals below establishment)	

Army Form C. 2118.

WAR DIARY
or
INTELLIGENCE SUMMARY
(Erase heading not required.)

M.H. Abriel Macdougall V.S. 90.
A.D.V.S. 46th (N.M.) Division
Page 8.

Place	Date	Hour	Summary of Events and Information	Remarks and references to Appendices
SAINS-EN-GOHELLE	29th April (contd)		Inspected animals of 3rd N.M. Fld Ambulance & Ax Noulette. They are in very good condition.	
	30th		The clipping of animals of the Divl Artillery is going on at the Horse Disl at BARLIN. Nearly all the artillery animals are put through. The weather has been warm & dry for the past week.	

J. M. Macdougall
A.D.V.S. Lt. Colonel
A.D.V.S. 46 (N. Midland) Division

Headquarters
46th (N.Mid) Division
Forwarded
J. M. Macdougall Lt. Colonel
A.D.V.S. 46. (N. Mid) Division

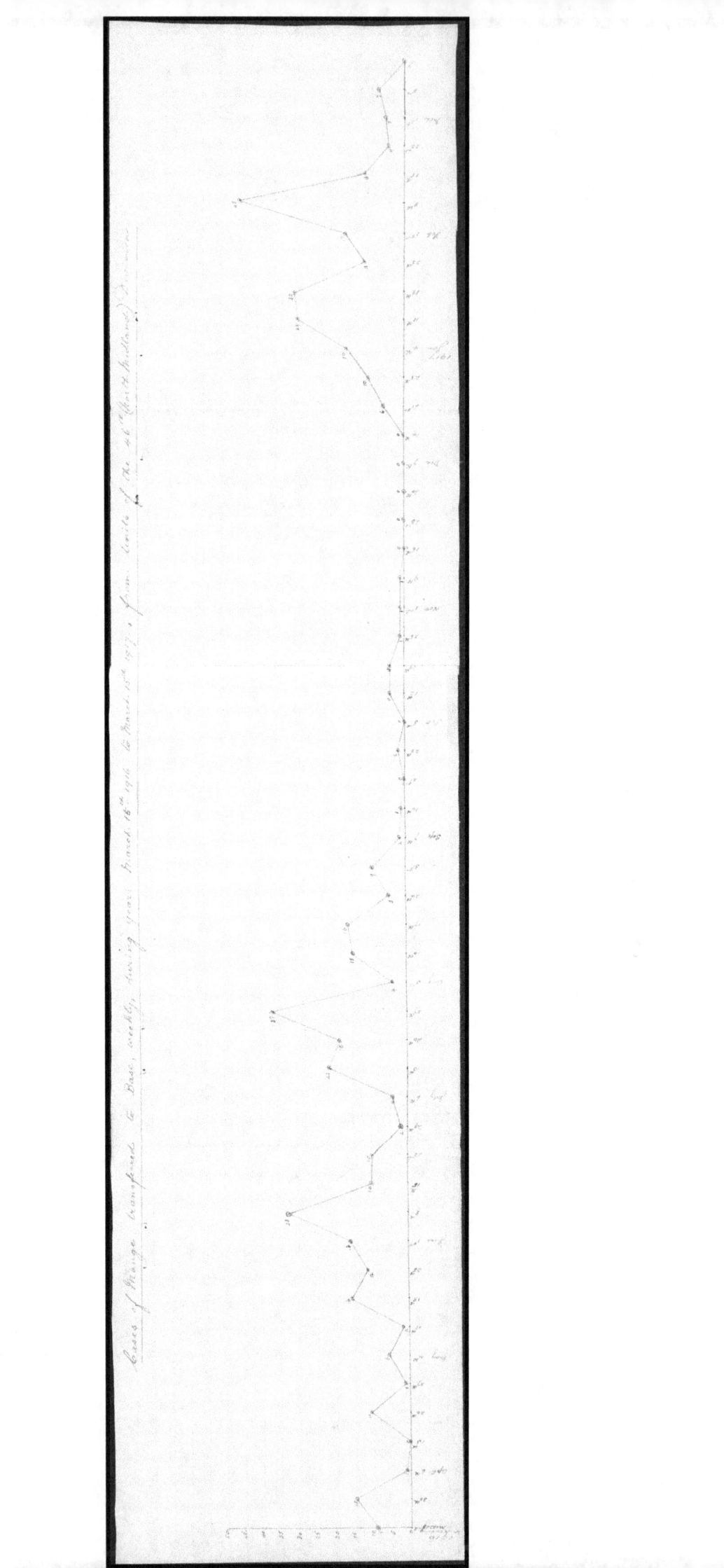

Cases of Mange eradicated weekly from herds of the U.S. Division during the year ending 15th June 1917.

Army Form C. 2118.

WAR DIARY
or
INTELLIGENCE SUMMARY of 1 A.O & 46th (North Midland) Division
(Erase heading not required.)

May 1917   Vol 23

Place	Date	Hour	Summary of Events and Information	Remarks and references to Appendices
SAINS-EN-GOHELLE	1st May		Went to Advan. Dep. at Berlin. The 3rd Canadian M.V.S. is moving transport from Berlin to environs forming & arrangement had to be made for returning the 46th Divl. Div Party employed at the Dep after the 3rd Canadian M.V. have.	
"	2nd "		Inspected 1/5 & 1/6 Coy R.E. - 1/1 Section 46th Bn. - 1st Ammunition Sub Park animals. 1/5th Coy R.E. = improving 1/6 " " = improving 1/1 Section 46 B.P. = good 1st Ammunition Sub Park = improving but the transport mules are not fit & are only getting 6 lb. oats. The officer (Ensn R – Rankin) left in charge is working to get them extra 6 lb. rate.	
"	3rd "		Inspected animals for evacuation at M.T.S. Mazingarbe. Inspected animals of 439 S. Coy A.S.C. which were very much improved. In condition. A.Q.1 The Gunnery officer A.D.C. officer of getting them.	
"	4th "		Petty Gunnery of V.O.	
"	5th "		Weekly Gunnery of V.O.	
"	6th "		Went to Berlin & saw Topt. Major & informed him that the 46th Div. was now fixed into the Army Corp attached officer of A.D.V. at office of D.D.V.S. First Army. Rode to No Bank de Laurette of Arras.	

Army Form C. 2118.

WAR DIARY
or
INTELLIGENCE SUMMARY
(Erase heading not required.)

A.D.V.S. 46th (N. Mid) Division

Place	Date	Hour	Summary of Events and Information	Remarks and references to Appendices
SAINS-EN-GOHELLE	May 4th		Inspected 139th M.O. Coy & sent seven horses to M.V.S. for Mange. A, B and C Batteries 231st Bgde R.F.A. & sent two horses of C Batty to M.V.S. for Mange & one case of Quitter from B/231. The horses seemed all inferior in condition with the a few exceptions, very thin in poor condition. One looking fairly well.	
"	8th		Inspected & field distributed 179 kerosite to Units of the Division. They were brought up from the Base by rail under the command of Captain Armitage A.D.S. and were distributed from D.A.S. Lines at HOUCHIN.	
"	9th		Inspected animals of 453rd, 454th and 451st Coys A.S.C. The animals are looking well in condition on the whole. Those of 451st & 454th Coys have seemed improved. The grooming in both Coys formerly that were growing is growing especially in 458 Coy. 453rd Coy A.S.C = 4 horses of cow to "working condition" 454th " " = 12 " " " " 451st " " = 12 " " " " (4 of 453rd Coy & 4 horses released from vehicles today & 2 front me feet not shooting [?] at 454th Coy. 12 of these animals are affected all over the body & the about without grub require	(2) of these animals had distention as they very emphisians of groins. Leaving 12 still without.

4/2449 W.t. W16937/Mgs 750,000 5/16 J.B.& L & N. Forms/C2118/32

WAR DIARY
or
INTELLIGENCE SUMMARY

Army Form C. 2118.

Place	Date	Hour	Summary of Events and Information	Remarks and references to Appendices
SAINS-EN-GOHELLE	9th May		Inspected Transport of 1st Field. U.S. at Barlin.	
"	10th		Inspected Transport of 138th Infantry Brigade, 4th Lincolns, 5th Lincolns, 4th Leicesters, 5th Leicesters, 4th Leicesters, 5th Leicesters at LES BREBIS. The condition of all 4 Reg'ts 488th U.O.A.S. 45th Leicesters at LES BREBIS. The condition of all satisfactory on the whole. The opportunity of addressing a letter was inspected & it to the influence of 137th Brigade. Signal centre, the former arranged to the latter for inspected animals for evacuation at H.Q. of field. W/c at BARLIN. the for of sun.	
"	11th		Inspected animals of 316 Road Construction Coy. R.E. at Fred. 10. & sent 240 tons in exchange of unsuitable for workers of V.b's.	
"	10.0 "		Weekly conference of V.b's.	
"			Inspected 68 & 88 Batteries 14th Army F.A. Bride. The tone of the & 88 are very good, now of the 82m Bty are not quite so good, but they are improving. Saw cases of [illegible] Wellston 88 Bty. on return to the charge of Major Barron, the Battery Commander. They are at Bony Sud. Fred. Ft. & Bty & Bry. E. north of Aix Noulette.	
"	13th "		Inspected the Mobile Veterinary Section from 68th Bty & Battery D. Battery = 2/3 Norman good. 1/3 Norman alt. Inventory Chimitry of training to sent Fred U.O. 1 Roan 2.D. with Manga on bolster. To be used by each officer.	

WAR DIARY
or
INTELLIGENCE SUMMARY
(Erase heading not required.)

Army Form C. 2118.

Place	Date	Hour	Summary of Events and Information	Remarks and references to Appendices
SAINS-EN-GOHELLE	13- May		A Battery = Improved - but many poor turnouts still. This Battery is concurrently poor throughout. B Battery = Horses fairly good. Men and Établis 2 cases thrush, went to D.T.S. C Battery = Fairly good. Men and Établis 1 case fever sent to All+S. Inspected animals for evacuation by M.V.S. Suspected cases of Officers and Sergeants A.V.C. of the Division on Anti-Gas. Evidence of horses: fair returns if a gas shell at the surroundings. Greyhound that can't run Nightmare (that died on a horse hide hours ago, and stopped with the recent) - Nore-Mark Positive.	
"	14- "		Inspected Lashios of A.B.+C Battries 23rd Regt. R.F.A sent 3 mange cases from C Battery to debility pens + 1 case M from B Battery to M.V.S. for evacuation. Inspected 3.0 + 11 B Col Heart and Mange cases to M.V.S.	
"	15- "		Greyhound Hunter 1 and 3 Sections 4.6 to 18.2.B. The foremen is satisfactory but Stallion tramways are light in condition, other perfect. — Considering to times of year, the light work &c.	

Place	Date	Hour	Summary of Events and Information	Remarks and references to Appendices

SAINS-EN-GOHELLE — May 16 — Captain W.G. THOMSON A.V.C. (T.F.) attached 231st Bde R.F.A. visited this Collar Horse yesterday afternoon on his way back from the Leave. Pte 465 Field Corporal R.E. at AIX NOULETTE & the Lines of 1st/1st & 1st/2nd Mid. Field Ambulances at FOSSE 10. His horse broke its knee two or three blocks back breaking its left collar bone, he was evacuated by the 1st/1st Mid. Field Ambulance to No 1 SCS at CHOCQUES.

Proceeded some supplies arrival of Lts 26 & 18 W. Spurrel R.G. spent leave to M.V.S. for Veterinary Reasons.

Went with P.A.D.V.S. to No 1 C.C.S. to see Captain W.G. Thomson, all to first arrangements & saw A.D.V.S.

17 PM — Inspected B and A Batteries 231st Bde R.F.A. Mr Lieut of Horses. The Horses of A Battery, of which A battery in comparison to the other Batteries, although thoroughly looked after & in fair little condition are, they are showing signs as of fatigue. Also — A visiting of Mogs — Regd Archt A or Lieut of Horses. The Horses of these Batteries are improving.

On the arrival of Reinforcements at 10 AM 18 in the afternoon —

18 — Weekly Conference of V.Os. — Only Capt F Dunkwart & Capt Shaw Fawn A.V.C.(T.F.) attended. Capt Mathison was transporting troops, Capt T Thomson was at No 1 CCS & Capt W.G. Thomson at this Collar Horse.

WAR DIARY or INTELLIGENCE SUMMARY

Army Form C. 2118.

Place	Date	Hour	Summary of Events and Information	Remarks and references to Appendices
SAINS-EN-GOHELLE	19th May		Officer in the morning inspected animals & Lines of 2nd Fd Amb. Field Ambulance at LEBUEVRIERE in the afternoon. The condition is satisfactory. Manes require trimming. All the animals are tied up with head-ropes, of pieces of wire instead of with chains. The letter being kept buried in sticky mud for the purpose, The A.D.M.S. was not present notwithstanding have the daily used for the purpose for which they are intended viz: tieing up the animals.	
"	30th		Inspected animals & lines of C Battery 236th Bgd R.F.A. at Bully GRENAY. Shot 2 horses to the M.V.S. for mange & suspected mange. two animals had been picked out to day before by Capt. S Farrar A.V.C.(T.F.) They were turned when these two arrived & when they were told to with caleine sulphide there kept in check & in consequence turned with calcium sulphide again with the advent of the warm weather. Two other poor mares related for the present with the Battery. Gun teams of this Battery is satisfactory. Went to 16th Fd. Amb. (Ambulance Stational & inspected in the afternoon.	
"	31st		Major Thomas A.V.C.(T.F.) reported his arrival from Cane to England. Inspected animals & prepared at M.V.S. 56 Anti-Air Corps Enforced for transfer redirected for each division. First Army R.A. Vty Order No. 950 dated 9th May 1917. Instructing AD.M.S. No. 6 B.A.T. for discharge to Q.O.C. L.& Division (A.O.) instructing the D.A.D.V.S. to investigate	

Army Form C. 2118.

WAR DIARY
or
INTELLIGENCE SUMMARY
(Erase heading not required.)

Instructions regarding War Diaries and Intelligence Summaries are contained in F. S. Regs., Part II. and the Staff Manual respectively. Title Pages will be prepared in manuscript.

Place	Date	Hour	Summary of Events and Information	Remarks and references to Appendices
SAINS-EN-GOHELLE	31st May 1917		To issue in accordance with it. By the 14/6/17 the I. Corps ordered 200 of the Reg'l drivers of 46th Division to be handed over to Ordnance Officer I. Corps. Troops put into use of I. Corps R.H.A. and Reserve Park. The I. Corps also ordered that the 14.=15 Fd. Arty 2. at present attached to the 46th Div'n was to leave in the morning of the following day. This necessitated a new distribution of the Mechanical T. staff submitted by me for approval of Divisional Commander & approved of.	
			6 Infantry Bgde M. Grs. — 10 per Regt.]	= 30
			18 " Batteries — 30 " Bty.	= 360
			4 Machine Gun Coys — 30 " Coy.	= 120
			3 Field Cos. R.E. — 25 " C.	= 75
			Signal Coy R.E.	= 15
			Pioneer Battalion	= 30
			Divisional Train	= 20
			Divisional M. Grs.	= 14
			R.A.M.C.	= 36
			3 Field Ambulances — 12 per 1 Ambulance	
			R.F.A.	
			230" Bgde R.F.A. — 4 Batteries — 40 per Battery	= 160
			231" " " — 4 " — 40 " "	= 160
			D.A.C. — 3 Sections — 40 per Section	= 120
			B.A.C. — 4 per Battery × 4 Batteries	= 16
				7500

WAR DIARY
or
INTELLIGENCE SUMMARY
(Erase heading not required.)

Army Form C. 2118.

Place	Date	Hour	Summary of Events and Information	Remarks and references to Appendices
SAINS EN GOHELLE	21 May 1918		Lectures & demonstrations on the use of Putrasaps of Anti Gas Embrocation for horses were given by the Divisional Officer of the Gas School to the MO's & certain Officers of the AVC & three other officers to assist the Senior NCO's of units. Instructors had been actively employed.	
"	22"	"	Inspected animals & lines of 453rd Cy A.S.C. Condition satisfactory. Sent one isolated horse to MVS for medical treatment.	
"	23"	"	Inspected animals of No 2 Section 46 # OAC. Condition & lines good. Tenderness on back some horses. Hair off ten mules. Took 2 off. Stared ford. Had lacker out & new to horses. Admitted that this had been so much dry seasoned as water was stopped.	
			Inspected 452nd Cy A.S.C. Condition good. Saddle sores sent to MVS for Treatment. Two horses died in knackage. Sent 3 knackage.	
			Inspected 457 " Cy A.S.C. Condition good. Sixty eight horses evacuated.	
			Inspected 454 Cy A.S.C. Condition good. Eight horses evacuated received from no. 2 Section of Range.	
			Inspected 1st Commutes. Intense work of infantry made any inspection impossible more than slight. M.V.S. in good order.	
"	27"	"	Inspected animals & lines M.V.S. & inspected Director of Veterinary Services Brigadier General E. Moore C.B. Inspected the M.V.S. at 11 A.M. Smyth Midland M.V.S. at 11/20 A.M. DO V.S. BARLIN Colliery at 11/30 A.M. A.V.S. were present. Major Drummond. Mess of following officers of A.V.C. were present: Lieut. Drummond, Lieut. Scott managing 1/5 H. Ho M.V.S. Captain E. Martley Commanding 1/15 H. Ho M.V.S. Captain F. Burkhart	

WAR DIARY or INTELLIGENCE SUMMARY

Army Form C. 2118.

Place	Date	Hour	Summary of Events and Information	Remarks and references to Appendices
SAINS-EN-GOHELLE	24th May		Captain T. Flannery, Captain John Facer, and Captain J. Bradley, attached to 14th Brigade Army, Field Artillery.	
"	25.		Inspected B Battery 23I. These R.F.A. lorries on their orders Lieut. Bruffles weekly Conference of V.Os. Only Capt. Bruffatt, T. Flannery & Facer present. Capt. G. Hartley has evacuated return, and Capt. W. G. Hannum reed. to England.	
"	26th		Inspected arrivals for Evacuation at M.V.S.	
"	27.		Attended Monthly Conference of A.D.V.S. at office of D.D.V.S. First Army.	
"	28.		Inspected arrivals in working orders for English range at 454th Cd. R.E. and new (no to M.V.S. as effects with the case united) M.V.S. & saw the cases which had been admitted since our last visit.	
"	29.		Inspected Co. & A Batteries 230th Bgde. R.F.A. Condition much improved. Sent one horse of G. Battery to M.V.S. for mange. This horse had turned at a manifest unsatisfactory recently that evidently been noted for the ? some time previously.	
"	30.		Lt. Colonel W. A. McDougall D.S.O. D.D.V.S. #VI.(a) Division proceeded to First Army Headquarters to act as D.D.V.S. First Army during the absence on leave of Colonel B. G. Ledger D.V.S. Captain G. Hartley MC (T.F.) joined 4.6 Div. D.V.S. to get as A.D.V.S. and Captain T. Flannery Ars (T.F.) proceeded to join 1st Vet. Emergency Compound to filled M.V.S. from Captain G. Hawkins ars (T.F.) from one other of 5 Veterans Ambuls. Harrieus ars(T.F.)	

Army Form C. 2118.

WAR DIARY
or
INTELLIGENCE SUMMARY of A.D.V.S. 46th (N.Mid) Division
(Erase heading not required.)

Instructions regarding War Diaries and Intelligence Summaries are contained in F. S. Regs., Part II. and the Staff Manual respectively. Title Pages will be prepared in manuscript.

Place	Date	Hour	Summary of Events and Information	Remarks and references to Appendices
SAINS EN-GOHELLE	30th May 1917		Capt. W.H. Magahlone A.V.C. T.F. reported his arrival by telephone at Houx-les-Mines. He was instructed to proceed to 230 Bgde R.F.A. wagon lines at Bully Grenay. Visited 230 Bgde R.F.A. wagon lines at Bully Grenay and visited round A.& D. Batts. Left Capt. Magahlone + Lt T.S. In the afternoon visited M.V.S.	

C Hartley
Capt A.V.C. T.F

2449 Wt. W14957/M90 750,000 1/16 J.B.C. & A. Forms/C.2118/12.

Army Form C. 2118.

WAR DIARY
or
INTELLIGENCE SUMMARY of #4 D.V.S.
(Erase heading not required.)

June 1917.

Vol 2

Place	Date	Hour	Summary of Events and Information	Remarks and references to Appendices
SOMME-SUR- SOMME	1/6/17		Monthly epidemic of K.O's. Capt T. Thomson A.V.C. was evacuating horses at Barlin and did not attend. Lt-Col W.O M.Dougall visited office during meeting	
	2/6/17.		Inspected 100 horses of 132 Inf. Coy at Les Brebis and sent them to M.V.S. for mange. In afternoon inspected isolated horses of #34 Coy A.S.C. and returned 100 to duty " #51 Coy A.S.C. " " #52 Coy A.S.C. none of which were sufficiently clean to make one case of Mange sent to M.V.S from this Company	
	4/6/17.		Inspected horses of #6th Divl H.Q.rs & #6 Divl Sigl Coy. Inspected Batn. H.Q.rs #1 D.A.C. Three animals sent instantly informing.	
	5/6/17.		Inspected 42 horses and 24 mules stationed in lines of 46th D.A.C. Auchen. one catarrh, one suspected mange & one ringworm case sent to M.V.S.	

Army Form C. 2118.

WAR DIARY
or
INTELLIGENCE SUMMARY

(Erase heading not required.)

A.D.V.S. 46th (N.M.) Division

June 1917

Place	Date	Hour	Summary of Events and Information	Remarks and references to Appendices
SAINS-EN-GOHELLE	2/6/17		Inspected animals of 466 A.T. Company R.E. One case of mange sent to M.V.S. and evacuated	
	5/6/17		Weekly conference of V.O.'s. Visited M.V.S. and inspected animals for mange.	
"	9/6/17		In office. Visited Section II 46th D.A.C. in afternoon.	
"	10/6/17		Inspected at 137 Inf. Bde. Horse Show at Marquillie's Farm.	
"	11/6/17		Lt. Colonel MacDougall D.S.O. joined 46th Divisional Headquarters from temporary duty at First Army Headquarters during the absence on leave of Colonel E.H. Curtis C.M.G. of A.D.V.S. First Army. Captain E. Hartley R.A.V.C. (T.F.) joined 1/1st North Midland M.V.S. from 46. Divisional Headquarters. Signed the Official Charges & N.C.O.'s journals that the treatment was satisfactory. Signed also Nos. 1388 & 1389 - Infantry Brigades at Marquillie's Farm.	
"	13/6/17		Inspected the treatment of horses in M.V.S. Attended divisional horse show in the afternoon.	
"	13/6/17		Visited the horses of I and D Batteries & 231 Brigade R.F.A. with Captain W.H. Macfarlane M.B. (77) at Bully-Grenay. Went to Captain W.H. Macfarlane to certain things to say Captain treat about and found him as to what ... ... satisfactory as regards to having received ... ... to give no cause for complaint. ... ... every tent to give no cause for complaint.	

Army Form C. 2118.

WAR DIARY
or
INTELLIGENCE SUMMARY

A.D.V.S. 46th (N. Mid) Division

(Erase heading not required.)

June 1917

Place	Date	Hour	Summary of Events and Information	Remarks and references to Appendices
SAINS-EN-GOHELLE	14/6/17		Col. Capt. C. Hartley A.V.C.(T.F.) Proceeded on leave to England for 10 days. Inspected horses of 6/23rd Bde R.F.A.	
"	15/6/17		Went to 457 Cav. A.V.S. at the request of O.C. 46th Amb Train received out from about 6 divns, tried to persuade them two which in my opinion should be shot, to that I Corps Horse Show on Wednesday the 18th instant. Also went to H.Q. Bn & Free Ho. O.P. Inspected animals at M.V.S. for evacuation.	
"	16/6/17		Sunday.	
"	17/6/17		I Corps Horse Show at DROUVIN Capt Glen Tracy A.V.C.(T.F.) Jumped. This was in the Open Jumping competition but was 4th placed. The evening was fairly fine. Heavy & frequent thunder showers & to bad weather was bad.	
"	18/6/17		Inspected A B and D Batteries 231st Brigade R.F.A. – A Battery = condition good, well groomed.	
"	19/6/17		I Inspected the horses of these Batteries and B " = condition fair & found by the Supt Veterinary which is available if not very well groomed. thought to be a start that with a morning to D " = condition fairly rough. send the animals to to be a see have grafting the Reg tr/ could be got. I returned via the stabling the dist to the tent OA supply lines. light rather than	

WAR DIARY or INTELLIGENCE SUMMARY

Army Form C. 2118.

Place	Date	Hour	Summary of Events and Information	Remarks and references to Appendices
SAINS-EN-GOHELLE	20/6/17	P.M.	Attended a Conference held by D.V.S. at No 23 Veterinary Hospital St OMER. - About 5 pm.	
"	21/6/17	8.30 A.M to 6 P.M	Rode over to I Corps H.Qrs at LABUISSIERS. Visited myself on A.D.V.S. I Corps re accidence with Headquarters I Corps (A.58/11/7 dated 8/6/17) and the Premium to A.2527/10 dated 19/6/17 arranged that D.A. & Q.M.G. Hqts General J.M. Anderson - that Medical Inquiry with 46th Division Motor next Tuesday 26/6/17 by which time A.P.V. North and (T.D) should have returned from Leave. Meantime I have ordered Sjt Goss Statutory Depot Pelham in certain articles of veterinary. In closing office of A.D. & S.T. Corps. Weekly Inspection of H.Q.O. - Present Captain Ruddiman, T. Ferguson & Mr Iorbaker, (Q.N. Mechanical) also Captain G. Bradley O.T. Off to 14 Corps to inspect Reviewed Officer G.G. Matter B.V.P. Regarding the two advanced cases of Mange in Horses & discussed with W.D.S. Pneumonia & arranged to expect Sjt Pt. in the Mattery tomorrow at 3 P.M. - They being furnished from units to Heavy Battery (S.A.A. Group) I Corps	
"	23/6/17		[illegible continuation]	Condition = Good Shoeing = Good Clipping = Nil Intelligence - Nil

WAR DIARY or INTELLIGENCE SUMMARY

Army Form C. 2118.

A.D.V.S. 46th Division

June 1917.

Place	Date	Hour	Summary of Events and Information	Remarks and references to Appendices
SAINS-EN-GOHELLE	23/6/17		Inspected teams of 136th Hy Battery, I Corps Heavy Artillery. Material = satisfactory. Shoeing = satisfactory. Shield = well groomed.	
	26/6/17		Lt. Col. W.A. M'c Dougall. D.S.O. proceeded to I Corps Hqrs to undertake the duties of A.D.V.S. I Corps.	
	27/6/17		Capt C. Hartley returned from leave to England and took over duties of D.A.D.V.S. 46th Divn with the rank of temporary Major.	
	28/6/17		Visited A.D.V.S. 1st Corps. In afternoon visited 46th M.M.V.S. and inspected horses for evacuation to V.g.C.	
	29/6/17		Weekly conference of V.O's. Present Captains F. Thomson, F. Shuttleworth, J. Facer, W.S. M'c Farlane and J. Bindley. A.V.C.	
	30/6/17		With Capt W.H. M'c Farlane I inspected a detachment of 9th Machine Gun Company at Bully Grenay. Sent two horses to M.V.S. for exhausted debilitance. Inspected 138 M.G. Coy and sent one mule to M.V.S. for Mange. The general condition of the animals is good. In afternoon visited C/23 & 10 X Batteries of 23rd Army Bgde R.F.A. at Rep. Noulette.	

C. Hartley, Major
D.A.D.V.S. 46th Div

WAR DIARY
or
INTELLIGENCE SUMMARY

Army Form C. 2118.

D.A.D.V.S. 46th Div.   July 1914

Place	Date	Hour	Summary of Events and Information	Remarks and references to Appendices
SAINS-EN-GOHELLE	1/7/17		Visited #61 - #52 - #64 Bdes A.S.C. and inspected horses which had been entailed as sufferers of skin disease. Sent 1 horse of #64 Bty & 2 horses of #51 Bty to M.V.S. on Mange. In morning inspected 46 D.H.Q. & 46th Div Signal Coy R.E. which both doing well.	
	2/7/17		Visited M.V.S. to arrange & feed. Inspected B.C. to Capture Front Ave. Inspected animals for evacuation.	
	3/7/17		Visited C/231 Bgde R.F.A. The horses much improved since last seen then. 3rd N.M. Fld Ambulance animals in good condition. Staffs mess horse improvement.	
BURTON	4/7/17		Moved to BURTON. First WM M.V.S. to BATUS. 46th Divl Artillery-remain in the line.	
	5/7/17		Visited all transport of 137 Inf Bgde & #53 Bty R.S.C. Sent to M.V.S. one mule & 1 horse from 6th NH Staffs. Condition of all animals good. All animals with exception of a few Bgde Hqrs & a few of 2/4 NH Staffs are in the open.	

2449 Wt. W14957/M90 750,000 1/16 J.B.C. & A. Forms/C.2118/12.

WAR DIARY
or
INTELLIGENCE SUMMARY

Army Form C. 2118.

D.A.D.V.S. 46th Division

July 1917.

Place	Date	Hour	Summary of Events and Information	Remarks and references to Appendices
CURATON	6/7/17		Conference of V.O.s. Only Capt. J. Fraser attended. Capt. E. Douthwaite on leave. Capts T. Thomson & Capt. W.H. Macfarlane have remained with 46th Div. Artillery. In afternoon took A.D.V.S. & Capt. to 5th Glens - 2nd N.M. Fd Ambulance - 3rd Glens Fd - 4th Leics Bde & 4/5 N.M. M.V.S.	
	7/7/17		Attended conference at office of A.D.V.S. Troops	
	8/7/17		Visited 46th Div. Signal Coy R.E. & at Monmouths - 452 Coy A.S.C.	
	9/7/17		Visited 4th Glens - 130th H.E. Bty and arranged to врид all animals with Calcium Sulphide - 5th Sherwoods - 454 Coy A.S.C.	
			In afternoon A.D.V.S. & Capt. inspected 2nd Monmouths & 475 G.I.C. Bty.	
	10/7/17		Office in morning. In afternoon A.D.V.S. & Capt. inspected 2nd Monmouths	
	11/7/17		Visited 137th Inf Bde, 1st N.M. Fd Ambulance & 453 Coy A.S.C.	

Army Form C. 2118.

WAR DIARY
or
INTELLIGENCE SUMMARY

(Erase heading not required.) O.A.D.V.S. 18th Div.

Instructions regarding War Diaries and Intelligence Summaries are contained in F. S. Regs., Part II. and the Staff Manual respectively. Title Pages will be prepared in manuscript.

July 1917.

Place	Date	Hour	Summary of Events and Information	Remarks and references to Appendices
BURTON	12/7/17		Inspected of 54 Coy A.S.C. Sent two animals to Vet. H.M. who for mange. Animals improved. A few them are being rested and turned out to graze. Visited of 52 Coy A.S.C. & 43rd Div Sig Coy R.E. In evening visited 1st Monmouths & 178 M.G. Coy. Conference of V.O.'s. Captain Facer attended.	
	13/7/17		Attended conference at A.D.V.S. I Corps.	
	14/7/17		Inspected horses of D.H.Q. Inspected dog belonging to cordon at MAGNICOURT which had bitten a man of of Lincolns. Found it healthy.	
	15/7/17		Visited A.D.V.S. I Corps. Inspected four horses of 452 Coy R.S.C. at LACONTE and seven horses of 451 Coy R.S.C. at BRAGEMONT. These animals were received as remounts on June 26th and had been the subject of an adverse report by O.C. H61st Vet Evn. It was stated that they were much improved and to-day they are in fair working condition. One animal in of 51 Coy A.S.C. is stated to be in a bad condition. Went on to GONNEHEM to see if remounts had arrived.	

WAR DIARY
or
INTELLIGENCE SUMMARY

Army Form C. 2118.

July 1917   D.A.D.V.S. #53rd Div.

Place	Date	Hour	Summary of Events and Information	Remarks and references to Appendices
CURTON	16/7/17		Inspected and distributed remounts at Gonnehem. 16 Chargers, 9 Riders, 132 L.D. 2 Mules, 13 Heavy Draught for #5 Division & 13 HD for 9. Reserve Park A.S.C. Chargers are moderate. Riders fair. L.D. manage considerably. Some old horses and a number of them show signs of having only recently recovered from Skin Disease. Riders were issued that they should be strictly isolated on arrival at units. HD Good. 8 animals were lame. Two unable to travel handed over to 9903 MVS. In afternoon visited #1st NMMVS.	
	17/7/17		Inspected #6.2 by A.S.C. Good. Visited #04 Coy A.S.C. & #6th Div Signal Coy RE. Visited DADVS 6th Div. to arrange for relief. Did not see him. In afternoon Lymkhana at DHQ. Coy't Races were anything comparison. Given Bending Race & Potato Race. Rained most of the time.	
	18/7/17		Visited # 52 - #54 Coys A.S.C. and inspected animals for examination that NMMVS. In afternoon by motor car visited 460 Fd Coy RE (Gorre then Annequin) 464 Fd Ambulance (Gorre) & 2nd NM Fd Ambulance (Gorre) that animals received for inspection then deceased	

WAR DIARY
or
INTELLIGENCE SUMMARY

Army Form C. 2118.

D.A.D.V.S. 46th Div.

July 1917

Place	Date	Hour	Summary of Events and Information	Remarks and references to Appendices
	20/7/17		Weekly conference of V.O's. Capts Faces & Southorate attended.	
	21/7/17		Attended conference at A.D.V.S. I Corps	
	22/7/17		Visited 459th Coy A.S.C. & 46th Div Signal Coy R.E. at LA COMTÉ.	
			Inspected 178 M.G. Coy. Condition of animals good.	
	23/7/17		Inspected animals at 4th N.M.M.V.S. for evacuation.	
	24/7/17		Inspected animals of 2nd N.M. Fld Ambulance at BETHUNE.	
SAILLY-LA-BOURSE	25/7/17		Moved to SAILLY-LA-BOURSE. Saw M.V.S. march into their billets at DROUVIN. Visited 3rd N.M. F Ambulance & 7th Sherwood Foresters.	
			Very heavy thunderstorm.	
	26/7/17		Visited units in SAILLY-LA-BOURSE and LA BOURSE. 139 N.Ir.F. Coy = 1 mule went to M.V.S. for Mange. All units in good shape but some standings required repair particularly 6th Sherwoods, 178 & 138 M.G. Coys.	

Army Form C. 2118.

WAR DIARY
or
INTELLIGENCE SUMMARY
(Erase heading not required.)

D.A.D.V.S. 46th Div   July 1917

Place	Date	Hour	Summary of Events and Information	Remarks and references to Appendices
SAILLY-LA-BOURSE	27/7/17		Went to Lorrechon to see remounts for 46th & 6th Divisions. Panels and 1 horse sent to M.V.S. with Mange. Several Horse remounts from lines of III Sector 6th D.A.C. In afternoon weekly conference of V.O's. Present Capts Irwin & Kenny 6th Division, Capt G.C. Thompson A.V.C. 147 Army Bde R.F.A. Capts T. Thomson F. Southwaite, J. Facer 46th Division	
	28/7/17		Visited dipping vat at Bethune. Remark of 4/2 N.M. F/M Ambulance and 4/5th Bde A.S.C. put through bath. Capt F. Southwaite A.V.C. T.F. in attendance.	
	29/7/17		Weekly conference at office of A.D.V.S. I Corps. Capt W.F. Thomson A.V.C. T.F. reported for duty from sick leave in England. He was posted to 2/31 Bde R.F.A.	
	30/7/17		Visited 1/466 Fld Coy R.E. at Noyelles and 468 Fld Coy R.E. at MAZINGARBE. In afternoon inspected 1/5th Coy A.S.C. Unit enjoying that two catsof	

Army Form C. 2118.

WAR DIARY
or
INTELLIGENCE SUMMARY
(Erase heading not required.)

D.A.D.V.S. 4th Div.

July 1917.

Place	Date	Hour	Summary of Events and Information	Remarks and references to Appendices
BARLY-AT-BOURSE	30/6/17		Range sent to M.V.S.	
	2/7/17		Inspected 21st-32nd-87th Batty's 2nd Bgde R.F.A and II Section 5th D.A.C. All good but 21st Batty has lost class of animal. D.A.D.V.S. From 7/7/17 the 70th Div Artillery have been administered by the 2nd Canadian Division. From 23/7/17 the 8th Div Artillery have been administered by me. The 2nd Bgde R.F.A has been administered by me from 29/7/17. The loss of one executive V.O. is severely felt, and it is almost impossible to give the care and attention to the units as formerly. I have found it necessary to do a certain amount of executive work as the V.O.'s could not have gone to all units particularly when in the rest area in which the Division were widely scattered.	

C. Hartley Major
D.A.D.V.S. 4th Div.

WAR DIARY
or
INTELLIGENCE SUMMARY

(Erase heading not required.)

Army Form C. 2118.

Vol 26
D.A.D.V.S. 46th Div.

Place	Date	Hour	Summary of Events and Information	Remarks and references to Appendices
BAILLY-LA-BOURSE	1/8/17		Capt. W. H. MacFarlane A.V.C.T.F. Left 231 Bde R.F.A to proceed to 12 V. Hospital Neufchatel.	
	2/8/17		Capt. F. Southwaite takes over temporary command of Vet N.M.M.V.S. vice Capt. F. Facet on leave to England. Visited M.V.S.	
	3/8/17		Conference of V.O.S. Present Capt. F. Southwaite 46th Div. Capt. Kennes and C/Sgt Macara Farrier S/M Dawson Capt & Andrew A/O 3rd Bde and Capt Kennes R.H.A. Visited tents in LA BOURSE with Capt Kennes	
	4/8/17		Conference at A.D.V.S. 1 Corps. Inspected animals of 1/2 N.M. Fd Ambulance. Superintended dipping of animals of 458 Coy A.S.C. 6 mules of 1/1 N.M.F.A. One mule of Battery sent sent to M.V.S. for mange. Visited M.V.S. & inspected animals for evacuation.	
	5/8/17		Inspected mares of 111 Battery R.F.A. before selection by remount committee.	
	6/8/17		Inspected 6th Sherwood Forester. 1 Mange v 1 suspected in contact sent to M.V.S. Visited 468 Field Coy and sent 1 Mange case to M.V.S. Visited 64th Nth Staffs and 139 M.G. Coy. Inspected two sets of harness belonging to Town Major	

WAR DIARY
or
INTELLIGENCE SUMMARY

(Erase heading not required.)

Army Form C. 2118.

D.A.D.V.S. H.Q 1st Div.

Place	Date	Hour	Summary of Events and Information	Remarks and references to Appendices
Sailly-Lau- Bourse	5/8/17		SANNY and found it in a very dirty condition. Arranged for it to be regularly cleaned.	
	6/8/17		Inspected horses of 4th Coy R.S.C. and sent one horse to M.V.S. for mange.	
	7/8/17		Saw animals for evacuation at 41st M.V.M.V.S.	
	8/8/17		Remount selection committee inspected mares of 6th Div R.A. with a view to branding those suitable for breeding.	
	9/8/17		Weekly conference of V.O's. Capt F. Douthwaite A.V.C. H., Capt Macara (Farrier) Henry & J. Andrew A.V.C. attended. In afternoon Remount Selection Committee inspected mares of 76th Div Infantry units.	
	10/8/17		Remount selection Committee inspected mares of H.Q. Army Brigade R.F.A. 2nd H.M. & 16th Field Ambulances.	
	11/8/17		Conference at A.D.V.S. I Corps.	
	12/8/17		Visited veterinary hospital and horses and sick evacuated. Inspected 58 F.M/2 R.E. Sent 1 mange case to M.V.S.	
	13/8/17		Inspected sick horses of 1st Bde Salvage But to M.V.S for Mange	

WAR DIARY
or
INTELLIGENCE SUMMARY

Army Form C. 2118.

D.A.D.V.S. 47th Div.

Place	Date	Hour	Summary of Events and Information	Remarks and references to Appendices
SAILLY-LA-BOURSE	14/8/17		Selected mares paraded at Château-des-Prés and branded TI on left cheek. 24 mags of 526th Divn R.26 & 6th Fd Coy R.E.s also chosen & branded TI on left cheek. Inspected animals of M. Flahaut for evacuation. Capt. J. Facer A.V.C. T.F. resumed command of 1/1st N.M.M.V.S. on return from leave.	
	15/8/17		Inspected selected animals at 2nd Cav Div Am. Col. & J Battery R.H.A. Sent 10 from former & 5 from latter unit to 1VS.	
	16/8/17		Animals of 1/37th Inf Bgde sent to Dipping Bath Bethune. Capt F Southwaite A.V.C. T.F. who was in charge sent animals home as only of the first dozen dipped were injured. None seriously.	
	17/8/17		Weekly conference of V.O.'s. Capts J. Facer, F Southwaite, C.P.S. Madara Evans, J.G. Kenny & J. Andrew & Lt. Shepton attended.	
	18/8/17		Conference at A.D.V.S. I Corps.	
	19/8/17		ADVS I Corps inspected 1/1e M.L. Coy, 5th South Staffs and 1st Monmouths	

Army Form C. 2118.

WAR DIARY
or
INTELLIGENCE SUMMARY
(Erase heading not required.)

D.A.D.V.S. 46th Div.

Place	Date	Hour	Summary of Events and Information	Remarks and references to Appendices
Army H.A.— Bouret	27/8/17		Visited 1st Monmouths. Inspected pack mules of 1st Monmouths with view to re-classification.	
	28/8/17		Weekly conference of V.O's. Inspected animals for evacuation at M.V.S.	
	28/8/17		Conference at A.D.V.S. 2 Corps.	
	29/8/17		Issued 45 remounts. 4 mules, food, to H.Q. First but some light in type.	
	27 L.D. Moderate. Two cases of Ophthalmia.			
	28/8/17		Visited 230 Bgde R.F.A. Inspected animals for evacuation at M.V.S.	
	30/8/17		Visited 231 Bgde R.F.A.	
	31/8/17		Weekly conference of V.O's. Inspected animals for evacuation at M.V.S.	

C Hartley Major
D.A.D.V.S. 46th Div.

Army Form C. 2118.

WAR DIARY
or
~~INTELLIGENCE SUMMARY~~
(Erase heading not required.)

Vol 27 D.A.D.V.S. 46th Division

Place	Date	Hour	Summary of Events and Information	Remarks and references to Appendices
SAILLY-LA-BOURSE	1/9/17		Visited #66 A.M. Fld Coy R.E. at MAZINGARBE. Horse lines shelled during the night. Found 12 dead & 20 injured (two were later destroyed). Three chargers of 137 Byde Hqrs also severely wounded.	
	2/9/17		Attended conference of A.D.V.S. I Corps in afternoon. Inspected Section III of #61st D.A.C.	
	3/9/17		Inspection of surplus animals by D.D.R. First Army. Animals sent to M.V.S. at Veity cross.	
	7/9/17		Weekly conference of V.O's. Attended conference of A.D.V.S. I Corps.	
	8/9/17		Inspected C/230 Bgde R.F.A.	
	9/9/17		Visited Sig Coy & Hqrt.	
	10/9/17		Capt T Thomson A.V.C.T.F. started on three weeks special leave to England	
	11/9/17		Visited units of 138 & 139 Inf Bgdes.	
	12/9/17		Inspected #52, #53, & #54 Coy A.S.C.	

Army Form C. 2118.

WAR DIARY
or
INTELLIGENCE SUMMARY.
(Erase heading not required.)

D.A.D.V.S. 76th Div.

Place	Date	Hour	Summary of Events and Information	Remarks and references to Appendices
SAILLY-LA-BOURSE	14/9/17		Weekly conference of V.O's. Inspected animals for evacuation at M.V.S.	
	15/9/17		Attended conference of A.D.V.S. I Corps.	
	16/9/17		Inspected animals for evacuation at M.V.S.	
	17/9/17		Inspected Sections I & II 76th D.A.C.	
	19/9/17		Weekly conference of V.O's. Inspected animals for evacuation at M.V.S.	
	21/9/17		Inspected 468 Fld Coy & 506 A.T. Coy R.E. at Noyelles. Attended conference at A.D.V.S. I Corps.	
	23/9/17		Inspected injured & slaughtered dogs at M. BAILEY, FERME DU CHATEAU NOYELLES.	
	24/9/17		Inspected D/230 & G/231 Bdes R.F.A. with A.D.V.S. I Corps. Inspected 1st Normandie.	
	25/9/17		Inspection of mares of 76th Div Artillery by Remount Selection Committee.	
	26/9/17		Weekly conference of V.O's.	
	27/9/17		Attended conference of A.D.V.S. I Corps.	
	29/9/17		Rebranded celated mares of 76th Div. Infantry.	
	30/9/17			

C. Hartley Major A.V.C. T.F.

Army Form C. 2118.

WAR DIARY
or
INTELLIGENCE SUMMARY.

(Erase heading not required.)

D.A.D.V.S. /46th Div.

WA 28

Instructions regarding War Diaries and Intelligence Summaries are contained in F. S. Regs., Part II. and the Staff Manual respectively. Title pages will be prepared in manuscript.

Place	Date	Hour	Summary of Events and Information	Remarks and references to Appendices
SAILLY-LA-BOURSE	1/10/17		Inspected animals at M.V.S. for evacuation. 12 remounts received from 23rd Div. Nine of them sent to M.V.S. as Veterinary cases.	
	2/10/17		With A.D.V.S. I Corps inspected Remounts from 46th Div afterwards evacted A/B/C 231 Bde R.F.A, A/B/230 Bde R.F.A & 46th F.A.C.	
	3/9/17		Visited various units with A.D.V.S. I Corps.	
	5/9/17		Inspected 13 animals at 6th D.S.C. for transfer to 46th Div.	
			Inspected animals for evacuation at M.V.S.	
	7/10/17		Took over duties of D.A.D.V.S. 46th (N.M) Division.	F.D.
	8.10.17		Met D.V.S. & party at the 11(N.M) M.V.S.	F.D.
	9/10/17		Visited the Tractor Lines of the 46th Div. & train.	F.D.
	10/10/17		11(N.M) M.V.S. moved to Skating Rink, Rue de Gendarmerie BETHUNE	F.D.
	"		Visited Remount Depot 1st Fd & with A.D.M.S. 46th Div to examine charger	F.D.
	"		Visited 46(2R.S., 4&5 Signal Div? 7&8 Quarter 46	
	"		17 animals evacuated this day cast by D.D.V.R. I Army, for veterinary reasons.	F.D.

Army Form C. 2118.

WAR DIARY
or
INTELLIGENCE SUMMARY.
(Erase heading not required.)

O.A.D.V.S. 46th Div.

Place	Date	Hour	Summary of Events and Information	Remarks and references to Appendices
PONY LA-BOURSE	11/10/17		Visited the 137th Inf.Bg.Transport Lines. Inspected animals at M.V.S. for evacuation. Reading Officers Wallet & Officers chest also 4 firing irons from Capt. C. Thompson A.V.C. attached 147 Army Brigade, R.F.A. Visited the 1st Monmouth Transport lines, also 466th R.E., D.H.Q. Div. & Signals	7 D.
	12/10/17			7 D.
	13/10/17		Visited 3 Coys of 46th Div Train. Supervised distribution of 194 Remounts.	7 D.
	14/10/17		Visited 137th Bgde Transport Lines & inspected remounts.	7 D.
	15/10/17		A.D.V.S. visited Sve arts Office & discussed about Evg hospital at Bethune.	7 D.
	16/10/17		Inspected Way feeding at 230th Brigade R.A. Battery R.F.A. for transfer to M.M.P. Service only. Issued to Divisional Artillery & D.A.P.V.S. by H.Q. 2 guards 465 Div. in connection with Evg Hospital at 1/1 N.M.M. M.V.S. Visited the Transport Lines of 452, 453, 454 Coys A.B.C.	7 D.
	17/10/17			7 D.
	18/10/17		Visited the 137th Inf.Bg Brigade,1 Monmouth & 178 M.G. Co Transport Lines.	7 D.
	19/10/17		Capt. F. Douthwaite A.V.C. T.F. returned to 46th Div Train. Assume duties of D.A.D.V.S. on return from 10 days leave in England.	
	20/10/17		Attended conference of A.D.V.S. I Corps.	
	21/10/17		Visited A/230 Bgde R.F.A. Interviewed F.O.C. R.F.A. with issue of obtaining tontead cake in lieu of straw for horses.	
	22/10/17		Visited D/230 - B 230 - C 230 Bgde R.F.A and #01 Coy A.S.C. whole lines	

WAR DIARY
or
INTELLIGENCE SUMMARY

Army Form C. 2118.

D.A.D.V.S. 46th Div.

Place	Date	Hour	Summary of Events and Information	Remarks and references to Appendices
SAILLY-LA-BOURSE	22/10/17		are being replaced by Chinese Labour Company. Ordered one horse to be clipped out for Ringworm. Animals have decidedly improved in condition since last seen. The trough which supplies water to C/230 Bgde & # 51 Coy Q.S.C. is under repair.	
	23/10/17		Visited 231 Bgde R.F.A. The animals of the Artillery Brigade have steadily improved since their arrival in the present area and much work has been done on the horse standings. A system of trace high clipping has been adopted and universally carried out. Some animals of C/230 and C/231 Bgde R.F.A. have been clipped out. During my absence on leave a segregation camp for Ophthalmia has been started at the M.V.S. to which horses of the Artillery are sent.	
	24/10/17		Visited # 6th D.A.C. Sections I v II	
	25/10/17		Visited # 52, # 53 v # 54 Coys Q.S.C.	
	26/10/17		Weekly conference of V.O.s. In afternoon inspected animals for evacuation at M.V.S.	

Army Form C. 2118.

WAR DIARY
or
INTELLIGENCE SUMMARY.
(Erase heading not required.)

D.A.D.V.S. 46th Div.

Instructions regarding War Diaries and Intelligence Summaries are contained in F. S. Regs., Part II. and the Staff Manual respectively. Title pages will be prepared in manuscript.

Place	Date	Hour	Summary of Events and Information	Remarks and references to Appendices
LILLERS-LA-BOURSE	27/10/17		Attended Conference of A.D.V.S. I Corps. Visited 1/2nd N.M. Fd Ambulance.	
	28/10/17		Capt. F. Douthwaite departed departure on 10 days leave of absence to England. Capt. T. Thomson takes over temporary charge of 1/6th Div. Train. I take over 137 Inf. Bgde, 1st Monmouth Regt, 1/8 M.T. Coy, & 466 Fd Coy R.E.	
	29/10/17		Visited 137 Inf Bgde.	
	30/10/17		Visited 139 Inf Bgde.	
	31/10/17		D.D.V.S. 1st Army inspected 1/1st N.M.M.V.S. & Gestakana Hospital. The animals of the division are in good condition. They are turned in good sheds with floors of brick or rammed chalk. The general health during the month has been good and there has been very little skin disease. The horses and some of the mules have been clipped out trace-high. There has been a great increase in the number of cases of Gestakana particularly among the R.A. Several forms of treatment are being tried and Lugol's solution at present appears to be given the most satisfactory results. C. Hartley Major A.V.C. T.F.	

Army Form C. 2118.

WAR DIARY
or
INTELLIGENCE SUMMARY.
(Erase heading not required.)

O.A.D.V.S. #6th Div.

Vol 29

November 1917

Place	Date	Hour	Summary of Events and Information	Remarks and references to Appendices
SAILLY-LA-BOURSE	2/11/17		Weekly conference of V.O's.	
	3/11/17		Attended conference of A.D.V.S. I Corps.	
	4/11/17		Visited D/231 Bde. R.F.A. to arrange for trial of zinc foot plates to prevent Pitre.	
	5/11/17		Visited A/231 Bde. R.F.A. & 5th & 6th Stationary Forestry Transport.	
	6/11/17		Visited B/230 Bde. R.F.A. & C and B/231 Bde R.F.A. with A.D.V.S. I Corps.	
	7/11/17		Inspection of animals for casting by D.D.R. Inspected animals for evacuation at M.V.S.	
	8/11/17		Visited #6 D.A.C.	
	9/11/17		D.V.S. inspected #1st N.M. M.V.S. Weekly conference.	
	10/11/17		Attended conference of A.D.V.S. I Corps. Inspection of horse mange by Remount Committee. Capt. F. Onthwaite A.V.C. NC returned from leave	
	11/11/17		Visited transport of 137 Inf. Bgde. Inspected animals for evacuation at M.V.S.	
	12/11/17		Inspected #51 Coy. A.S.C.	
	14/11/17		Visited 231 Bgde. R.F.A.	
	15/11/17		Inspected & distributed 31 remounts. Loud shoes for Artillery. Boots to Infantry.	

Army Form C. 2118.

WAR DIARY
or
INTELLIGENCE SUMMARY.
(Erase heading not required.)

D.A.D.V.S. 46th Div.

Place	Date	Hour	Summary of Events and Information	Remarks and references to Appendices
SAILLY LA-BOURSE	18/11/17		Weekly conference of V.O's.	
	19/11/17		Attended conference of A.D.V.S. I Corps. Lectured at R.A.M.C. school at No 33 C.C.S. on horse mastership.	
	20/11/17		Gave demonstration to class from R.A.M.C. school at 46th M.M.V.S.	
	21/11/17		Inspected forward section of S.A.S. section 46th D.A.C.	
	22/11/17		Visited A & C/230 Bde R.F.A.	
	23/11/17		Inspected Section 10", 46th D.A.C. Both good.	
	23/11/17		Weekly conference of V.O's.	
	24/11/17		Attended conference of A.D.V.S. I Corps.	
	25/11/17		Case of Stomatitis Catarrosa at 266 F.A. Co. R.E. on remount recent 15/11/17.	
	26/11/17		Inspected & distributed 49 remounts. Fair quality.	
	29/11/17		Preliminary inspection of animals for D.D.V.S. costing party.	
	30/11/17		Weekly conference of V.O's.	

C. Hartley
Maj. D.A.D.V.S. 46th Div.

Army Form C. 2118.

WAR DIARY
or
INTELLIGENCE SUMMARY.

(Erase heading not required.)

Instructions regarding War Diaries and Intelligence Summaries are contained in F.S. Regs., Part II. and the Staff Manual respectively. Title pages will be prepared in manuscript.

December 1917.

D.A.D.V.S. H.Q. VI Corps.

Place	Date	Hour	Summary of Events and Information	Remarks and references to Appendices
SAULTY	1/12/17		Attended conference of A.D.V.S. I Corps. Lectured on horsemastership to R.A.M.C. school, 33 C.C.S. in afternoon.	
LA BOURSE	2/12/17		Gave practical demonstration to Class from R.A.M.C. school at M.V.S.	
	4/12/17		Visited #66 Field Coy. R.E., 1st Monmouths & 1/4 Leicesters. Capt W. G. Thomson S.V.C. goes on leave to England for 14 days.	
	5/12/17		Visited 178 M.G. Coy, 139 Bde H.Qrs, 139 M.G. Coy & 6th Signal Coy R.E.	
	6/12/17		Visited Casting Parade for D.D.R. 1st Army. 8 animals cast.	
	6/12/17		Visited #65 Field Coy R.E. & forward section of S.A.A section #8th D.A.C. Weekly conference of V.O's.	
	7/12/17		Inspected #51 Coy R.A.S.C. Animals in good condition.	
	8/12/17		Attended conference of A.D.V.S. I Corps.	
	9/12/17		Inspected B/280 Bde R.F.A. One animal had been evacuated for mange. Two were put aside to be clipped. A very good battery.	
	10/12/17		Inspected animals for evacuation at M.V.S.	
	11/12/17		A.D.V.S. I Corps visited whole of the Artillery except sections II & III #65 D.A.C. Inspected A/281 Bgde. Satisfactory.	

Army Form C. 2118.

WAR DIARY
or
INTELLIGENCE SUMMARY.
(Erase heading not required.)

D.A.D.V.S. 46th Divn.

Instructions regarding War Diaries and Intelligence Summaries are contained in F. S. Regs., Part II. and the Staff Manual respectively. Title pages will be prepared in manuscript.

Place	Date	Hour	Summary of Events and Information	Remarks and references to Appendices
SAILLY-LA-BOURSE	12/12/17		Visited 137 M.G. Coy, 5th North Staffords, 137 Bgde H.Qrs.	
	13/12/17		Distributed 10 R.H L.D & 3 H.D remounts on mud road between NOEUX-LES-MINES & HOUCHIN. It was not advisable to take them into the lines of 453 Coy R.S.C. which were being shelled at the time. Inspected animals for evacuation at M.V.S.	
	14/12/17		Visited 468 F.H Coy R.E, 8th Sherwoods. Weekly conference of V.O's.	
	15/12/17		Attended conference of A.D.V.S. & Capts, visited M.V.S. & inspected mules of Section 1, 46th D.A.C. which were being clipped out. Made arrangements for clipping bath.	
	17/12/17		Visited S.A.A. Section 46th D.A.C, 465 Field Coy R.E, 566 Hants A.T.Coy R.E, 116 Labour Coy.	
	18/12/17		Visited 58, 60, 61st Batteries 14th Bgde C.F.A which are temporarily attached 60th Battery. Horse foot and 6 isolated for suspected skin disease. Fact. 1 Mange case sent to M.V.S. Ford.	

Army Form C. 2118.

WAR DIARY
or
INTELLIGENCE SUMMARY.
(Erase heading not required.) DADVS #6th (N.M.) Division

Instructions regarding War Diaries and Intelligence Summaries are contained in F. S. Regs., Part II. and the Staff Manual respectively. Title pages will be prepared in manuscript.

Place	Date	Hour	Summary of Events and Information	Remarks and references to Appendices
SAINY-LA-BOURSE	19/12/17		Visited Sections I & II, #6th D.A.C. Food condition but a few animals required more grooming.	
	20/12/17		Visited 6th South Staffs, 6th South Staffs, 6th Sherwoods, 2nd N.M. F.A. Capt W. F. Thomson returned from leave. Weekly conference of V.O.'s.	
	21/12/17			
	22/12/17		Placing tanks of I Corps Dipping Bath destroyed by enemy bomb & remainder of 4th Division shed were awaiting evacuation were killed. Visited A.D.V.S. I Corps to report on disease situation.	
	23/12/17			
	26/12/17		Inspected & received 169 remounts from lines of section 1 #6th D.A.C. Riders hoot. L.D. & H.D. of medium quality. Capt F. FACER on leave to England. Capt T. Thomson took over Employ Command of 4th N.M.M.V.S.	
	27/12/17		Visited #61 #62 #63 Coys A.S.C. One mange case sent from #63 Coy to A.V.S.	
	28/12/17		Preliminary casting parade of remount cases Weekly conference A.D.V.S. I Corps	
	29/12/17		Attended conference of A.D.V.S. I Corps.	

C. Hartley Major AVCTE

Army Form C. 2118.

WAR DIARY
or
INTELLIGENCE SUMMARY.
(Erase heading not required.)

D.A.D.V.S. #6th Div. Vol 31

Instructions regarding War Diaries and Intelligence Summaries are contained in F. S. Regs., Part II. and the Staff Manual respectively. Title pages will be prepared in manuscript.

January 1918

Place	Date	Hour	Summary of Events and Information	Remarks and references to Appendices
SAILLY-LA-BOURSE	1/1/18		Sled with Walker eleven horses of 178 N.Z.Coy, which had joined unit from England.	
	2/1/18		Visited 230 Bgde R.F.A.	
	4/1/18		Weekly conference of V.O.s.	
	5/1/18		Attended conference of A.D.V.S. I Corps.	
	10/1/18		Mange Bath at Bethune started. Horses of A/230 Bgde R.F.A. were put through it also 57 animals of B/230 Bgde R.F.A. Weekly conference of V.O.s.	
	12/1/18		159 horses of D/230 Bgde R.F.A. & 85 of B/230 Bgde R.F.A. passed through Mange Bath. Attended conference of D.D.V.S. I Corps.	
			Inspected & distributed 51 remounts from Lines of Section 1. 46th D.A.C. Verquigneul	
	17/1/18		Weekly conference of V.O.s. to be held in future each Thursday afternoon	
	18/1/18		A/231 & C/231 Bgde R.F.A. put through Mange Bath.	
	19/1/18		Attended conference of A.D.V.S. I Corps.	
LA BEUVRIERE	23/1/18		Moved to LA BEUVRIERE.	
	24/1/18		Weekly conference of V.O.s.	
	25/1/18		Visited 139 Inf. Bgde.	
	26/1/18		Attended conference of A.D.V.S. I Corps. & Lecture on Horsemastership by Col. Millet at I Corps H.Q.rs.	

Army Form C. 2118.

WAR DIARY
or
INTELLIGENCE SUMMARY.

(Erase heading not required.)

D.A.D.V.S. 46th Div.

January 1918.

Place	Date	Hour	Summary of Events and Information	Remarks and references to Appendices
LA BEUVRIERE	28/1/18		Visited 4th Lines & 1st Monmouths	
	29/1/18		Visited 230 Bgde R.F.A. 5th & 6th Nth Staffs.	
			In the new area there is a shortage of land accommodation for animals. The majority of them are under cover but the floors are nearly all bad and require repair.	

Chalton
Maj. AVCTF.
D.A.D.V.S. 46th Div.

D.A.D.V.S.
46TH.
GEN. DIVISION.
3.2.18

Army Form C. 2118.

WAR DIARY
or
INTELLIGENCE SUMMARY.
(Erase heading not required.)

D.A.D.V.S. 46th Div.

February 1918.

Place	Date	Hour	Summary of Events and Information	Remarks and references to Appendices
LA BEUVRIERE	1/2/18		Inspected #53 Coy A.S.C. & 2nd N.M. Fld Ambulance. Both good but the animals of the latter unit were looking rough & untidy. Visited 1 V.S. and inspected animals for evacuation.	
	2/2/18		Attended conference of A.D.V.S. 2 Corps & visited 1st N.M. Field Ambulance.	
	3/2/18		Visited 5th, 6th, 7th, 8th Sherwood Foresters.	
	5/2/18		Visited Bomy area preparatory to taking over.	
	7/2/18		Weekly conference of V.O.s	
	8/2/18		Inspected horses for evacuation at 1/1st & 1/1 N.M.V.S.	
	9/2/18		Marched to Bomy. Office at Billet 28	
	11/2/18		Inspected and detailed remounts from Beaumetz-les-Aire	
	12/2/18		Visited 301 v 113 96th D.A.C. All animals in the open under exposed conditions	
	14/2/18		Inspected 1st Squadron Mounted Traffic Control	
	15/2/18		Inspected animals for evacuation at 1/1st N.M. V.S.	
	18/2/18		Visited 230 Bgde R.F.A. Practically all animals were in the open in exposed conditions. Some breed in condition but the horses were looking as well as could	
	19/2/18		Farm visits. be expected	

Army Form C. 2118.

WAR DIARY
or
INTELLIGENCE SUMMARY.
(Erase heading not required.)

D.A.D.V.S. 4th Res

February

Instructions regarding War Diaries and Intelligence Summaries are contained in F. S. Regs., Part II. and the Staff Manual respectively. Title pages will be prepared in manuscript.

Place	Date	Hour	Summary of Events and Information	Remarks and references to Appendices
Bony	1/2/18		Weekly meeting of V.O's	
	2/2/18		Visited S.A.A. Section 76th D.A.C. Sa Gehan Evolution of animals satisfactory	
	24/2/18		Visited AOVS 2 Coys & # 51 & # 57 Bys A.C.C.	
	27/2/18		Visited 1st Lincs, 1st Lancaster, 130 & 189 M.G. Coys, Cx D Batteries 100 Byde RFA with I Corps Horsemasters	
	28/2/18		Inspected & distributed remounts	

C. Hartley
Major A.V.C.F.

WAR DIARY
or
INTELLIGENCE SUMMARY.

Army Form C. 2118.

D.A.D.V.S. 46th Division.

VII 33

Place	Date	Hour	Summary of Events and Information	Remarks and references to Appendices
BOMY.	3/3/18		#6th D.H.Q moves to FOUQUIERES-LES-BETHUNE.	
FOUQUIERES	4/3/18		Made arrangements for 9/6st H.M.M.V.S. to have billet at Rue de la Gendarmerie BETHUNE with No 22 M.V.S. It is impossible to get another billet as the area is so crowded.	
	5/3/18		Visited 137 Inf. Bgde Wagon Lines in LE PREOL. All animals in good cover but some of the lines are rather near Battery positions for safety. 138 Inf. Bgde lines are good. Bomb D/231 Wagon lines are engaged on BEUVRY. C/231 & A/231 Bgde R.F.A. in good lines on Bethune road. The animals seen appear to have stood the march well.	
	6/3/18		Visited A, C & D 230 Bgde R.F.A. in ANNEZIN & VENDIN. All in good cover. # 52 & # 63 Bgde A.S.C. in good cover at VENDIN & 51 Bgde A.S.C. at ANNEZIN. Majority of animals under cover. Hgrs and section of 76th D.A.C. at VENDIN. All mules in open. Condition of animals is on the whole satisfactory.	
	7/3/18		Visited #6 Div. M.F. Battalion and made arrangements with T.O. for sick lines sick line orderly etc. Weekly conference of V.O.s. Capt T. Thomson A.V.C. H. Leave to England	

Army Form C. 2118.

WAR DIARY
or
INTELLIGENCE SUMMARY.

(Erase heading not required.)

D.A.D.V.S. 46th Div.

Month: March

Place	Date	Hour	Summary of Events and Information	Remarks and references to Appendices
FOUQUIERES LES-BETHUNE	8/3/18		Visited Horse line 906 at LE QUESNOY, now occupied by 420 Fd Coy R.E. to enquire as to its safety as it had been badly infected with Mange. Found that it had been thoroughly disinfected and the outbreak stopped. In afternoon inspected section 906-908 at ANETTES. Animals in good condition. Shoeing fair, some feet too long.	
	9/3/18		Conference at A.D.V.S. I Corps. Inspected animals for evacuation at M.V.C.	
	10/3/18		Inspected # 51 Coy A.S.C. Condition good, grooming indiff. Shoeing good except for tendency to "dump". Saw team horses of 84 A.F.A. Bde at same time. Condition fair.	
	11/3/18		Inspected # 62 Coy A.S.C. at VENDIN. Good. The water supply for all animals in this village is unsatisfactory. Saw # 46th D.A.C. Condition fair to good. Most of animals in the open and looking rough.	
	12/3/18		Visited 1/1st N.M.F.M.Ambulance. Satisfactory. 2nd N.M.F.M.Ambulance. Condition good but animals were unclipped. 3rd N.M.F.M.Ambulance. Condition indiff. & grooming fair.	

Army Form C. 2118.

WAR DIARY
or
INTELLIGENCE SUMMARY.
(Erase heading not required.)

March 1918.   D.A.D.V.S. 61st Div.

Place	Date	Hour	Summary of Events and Information	Remarks and references to Appendices
FOUGUERES	13/3/18.		Inspected 1st Monmouths. Satisfactory. Shoes thin but felt & heat.	
	14/3/18.		" #373 Coy ASC. at VERDON Very good.	
	15/3/18.		" A/231 Bde RFA Broken fact Shoeing done cold & needs improvement.	
			Weekly conference of V.O's.	
	16/3/18.		Visited 5th NR Staffs. Condition very good but animals in far too close proximity to gun positions. Recommended their removal. 6th NR Staffs very good. 8th NR Staffs were being moved from their sites to gun positions. Animals had lost condition owing to restlessness on last site. Inspected A + C/231 Bde RFA. Satisfactory.	
			Attended conference of A.D.V.S. & Vets.	
	18/3/18.		Inspected 2/6 (City) F.A by R.E. A much improved unit in excellent condition	
	19/3/18.		Inspected 1/6 Div. M.G Battalion. Condition fair to very good. 1 Mallet (Sgt sice to be condemn)	

Army Form C. 2118.

WAR DIARY
or
INTELLIGENCE SUMMARY.
(Erase heading not required.)

D.A.D.V.S. 4th Div.

Month: March

Place	Date	Hour	Summary of Events and Information	Remarks and references to Appendices
FOUQUIERES	19/3/18		Inspected & distributed remnants (?) Mules good. Horses moderate Issues of Vitaline. Inspected C/230 Bde. R.F.A. Condition & grooming good except that doors were not clean. D/230 Bde R.F.A. Condition fair to good. A few thin horses. Grooming fair.	
	20/3/18		Visited S.A.A. Section 4th D.A.C. Mules fit & clean but very rough & unkempt in coats & looking light.	
	21/3/18		Weekly conference of V.O.s	
	22/3/18		Inspected animals for evacuation at M.V.S. Attended conference of D.V.S. at LINERS in afternoon	
	23/3/18		Capt. T. Thomson returns from leave	
	24/3/18		Weekly conference of V.O.s	
	25/3/18		Moved to BRACQUEMONT. Look over administration of 176 A.B. R.F.A.(W.O.) (Lieut Connolly) & 241 A.B. R.F.A. (W.O. Bgd. (?) Hearne), and a number of small units	

WAR DIARY
or
INTELLIGENCE SUMMARY.

Army Form C. 2118.

D.A.D.V.S. 46th Div.

Month: March

Place	Date	Hour	Summary of Events and Information	Remarks and references to Appendices
BRACQUEMONT	31/3/18		Inspected B/126 Army Bde R.F.A. Horses foot Mules foot Shoeing satisfactory. The animals of the division all in good condition and have been helped by the fine weather and the fact that most of the units have been in good lines.	

C. Hartley
Major
D.A.D.V.S. 46th Div.

WAR DIARY
or
INTELLIGENCE SUMMARY.

Army Form C. 2118.

D.A.D.V.S. 46th Div.

Place	Date	Hour	Summary of Events and Information	Remarks and references to Appendices
BRACQUEMONT	1/4/18		Inspected 126 Army Bde R.A. Horses fair to good. Stables good but disinfectants wanted, rats in lofts. Shoeing good. Grooming not good.	1. Disinfectants wanted in lofts. Cheyne went to Divisional HQ.
	2/4/18		Many have had lice. Animals unproved round backs and thighs.	
			Visited 230 Bde R.F.A. Generally good. A Battery below the others.	
	3/4/18		Weekly conference of V.O.'s. Visited 468 F.A. Coy R.E. V.G.	
	4/4/18		Attended conference of A.D.V.S. I Corps.	
	5/4/18		Inspected C/242 Bde R.F.A. 56 Mange cases v.i. Reilly sent to M.V.S.	
	6/4/18		Attended D.D.V.S's inspection of animals for casting for remount meters.	
	9/4/18		Inspected 137 Inf Bde. at CAPENCY. V.G.	
BRAY	13/4/18		Moved to BRAY. The division coming out of action.	
	17/4/18		Cases of Epizootic Lymphangitis discovered on a large mule (remount 30/3/18) in section 1 46th D.A.C. Animal destroyed and all precautions taken.	
	23/4/18		D.D.V.S. inspected 46th D.A.C.	

Army Form C. 2118.

WAR DIARY
or
INTELLIGENCE SUMMARY.
(Erase heading not required.)

D.A.D.V.S. H.C. Div.

April 1918

Instructions regarding War Diaries and Intelligence Summaries are contained in F. S. Regs., Part II. and the Staff Manual respectively. Title pages will be prepared in manuscript.

Place	Date	Hour	Summary of Events and Information	Remarks and references to Appendices
Etaples	29/4/18		Moved to COSNAY	
COSNAY	23/4/18		Weekly meeting of V.O's. Took over administration of 3rd Army Corps R.F.A. V.O. 4/c Capt Whitton A.V.C.	
	25/4/18		Inspected 231 Bgde R.F.A. Food except D Battery.	
	26/4/18		Inspected 230 Bgde R.F.A. A Battery not satisfactory.	
	27/4/18		Inspected 81st Batty 3rd A.Bgde R.F.A. Poor to fair	
			Y/3 (How) Batty 3rd " Fair to good	
			G4 " Batty Fair	
			D/5 R.B. Poor to fair. The worst unit	

E. Huntley
Major
D.A.D.V.S. H.C. Div.

List of Units attached to 46th Division in Lens Sector

Unit	Location	Horses	Mules
9th Chinese Labour Coy	COUPIGNY	2	—
1st A.T. Coy Canadian E.	Q.12.a.1.4.	25	
Can Corps Gas School	Q.11.c.9.1	3	
Engineers Pool	COUPIGNY		
7th Bn Tank Corps	SAINS EN GOHELLE	5	
B & O Special Coy RE	" " "	2	2
77th Labour Coy	COUPIGNY	5	
2nd Garr Bn Ox & Bucks L.G. Coy	"	1	
331st Road Construction Coy	AIX NOULETTE (R.22.a.9.9)	8	10
No. 2 Sect Can Corps Tramway Coy	" "	2	
148 A.T. Coy RE	MARQIEFFLES Fme (R.26.d.3.7)		
324th Quarry Coy	" R.26.a.10.5		
10th Balloon Sect	X.3.d.3.5.	2	
1st Pontoon Pk RE	BARLIN	53	
3rd Aust Tunnelling Coy	BRACQUEMONT	10	
89th Labour Coy	GRENAY	3	
K & P Special Coys RE	BULLY GRENAY		4
126 Army Bde R.F.A. v/o L/h G Connolly a/c	BRACQUEMONT & NOEUX LES MINES	626	245
242 Army Bde R.F.A. v/o Capt C.G. Hearn a/c	SAINS-EN-GOHELLE & FOSSE DUPONT	622	229

Vol 5
Army Form C. 2118.

WAR DIARY
or
INTELLIGENCE SUMMARY.
(Erase heading not required.)

D.A.D.V.S. 46th Div.

May 1918.

Place	Date	Hour	Summary of Events and Information	Remarks and references to Appendices
Cosnay	1/5/18		Weekly conference of V.O's. Sgt Tarbutt A.V.C. T.F. attached 139 Inf Bgde reported sick, and evacuated to C.C.S.	
	3/5/18		Inspected 46th M.G. Battalion. Lines in Bois des Montagnes. Watering not very good. Condition of animals satisfactory. O.C. Company informed. Sgt Farmer taken over duties and has charge of wallet.	
	4/5/18		Attended conference of A.D.V.S. I Corps. Inspected 5th & 6th mob. Vetsections. Condition good. Sick animals are going down and are not being cared for as they should be.	
	6/5/18		Visited 1/3 N.M. F.d. Ambulance Lines. Inspected horse imported for transport to f.b.s. Battalion H.S. & Cpls. Not suitable as it has thrown harness. Indicated 9 animals at M.V.S. for evacuation.	
	7/5/18		Indicated two mules of Section 1. to be cast for vice. One pony to M.V.S. Other to be kept owing to Grijsotic lymphangitis having occurred in unit.	

Army Form C. 2118.

D.A.D.V.S. VI Co.

WAR DIARY
or
INTELLIGENCE SUMMARY.

(Erase heading not required.)

May 1918

Place	Date	Hour	Summary of Events and Information	Remarks and references to Appendices
Cassny	2/5/18		Inspected 136th Inf Bgde. in open in Bois des Montagnes. Good generally. Mules of 4th Leicesters & Horses of 5th Leicesters need a little improvement. Horse masters generally good throughout.	
	3/5/18		Inspected wagon lines at T.M.O. dist 36 B. In open Field muddy. #66 N.M Field Coy R.E. Wholes are satisfactory. Horses have lost some condition and are backward in their coats. #65 N.M Field Coy R.E. Satisfactory. Steadily improving. #61 Coy A.S.C. Improving. Satisfactory. #62 Coy A.S.C. Lines bad. Some horses have lost condition. #63 Coy A.S.C. Satisfactory. Bad lines. #54 Coy A.S.C. Good. Inspected animals for evacuation at M.V.S. In good condition & well looked after. All under cover.	
	9.5.18		Weekly conference of V.O.'s.	

Army Form C. 2118.

WAR DIARY
or
INTELLIGENCE SUMMARY.

(Erase heading not required.)

D.A.D.V.S. 46th Div.

May 1918

Instructions regarding War Diaries and Intelligence Summaries are contained in F. S. Regs., Part II. and the Staff Manual respectively. Title pages will be prepared in manuscript.

Place	Date	Hour	Summary of Events and Information	Remarks and references to Appendices
GOSNAY	10.5.18		Inspected L.D. ch. mare of B/231 Bgde R.F.A. for transfer to 46th Battn M.G. Corps.	
	11.5.18		Attended conference of A.D.V.S. I Corps.	
	13.5.18		Inspected 4 horses ridden by Chaplains for transfer to other units. Three suitable, one unsuitable. Capt. F. Deathorate A.V.C. 46 proceeded on final leave to England. Inspected Section I 46th D.A.C. Satisfactory. Mules better than horses.	
	14.5.18		Inspected Section II 46th D.A.C. Satisfactory.	
	15.5.18		Inspected S.A.A. Section 46th D.A.C. Good. Improved since last seen.	
	17.5.18		Inspected C/230 Bgde R.F.A. Good except for 15 to 20 animals. Fair to good. A.D.V.S. I Corps present. D/230 Bgde R.F.M. Learning letter and horses looking more fit. A/230 Bgde R.F.A.	
	16.5.18		Weekly Meeting of R.O.'s	
	17.5.18		Inspected H/231 Bgde Good. D/231 Bgde R.F.A. Improved but not up to standard. A.D.V.S. I Corps present.	

Army Form C. 2118.

WAR DIARY
or
INTELLIGENCE SUMMARY.
(Erase heading not required.)

MAY 1918.   DADVS 46th Div

Instructions regarding War Diaries and Intelligence Summaries are contained in F. S. Regs., Part II. and the Staff Manual respectively. Title pages will be prepared in manuscript.

Place	Date	Hour	Summary of Events and Information	Remarks and references to Appendices
Gomay	18/5/18		Visited M.V.S. which was fitting on Range 17.	
	23/5/18		A.D.V.S. I Corps. Attended farriery conference of C.R.E. & Captain Hunter M.C. R.E.	
	24/5/18		Captain E. Donthwaite returned from leave	
	20/5/18		Inspected 1/1 N.M. Fd. Ambulance Good	
	21/5/18		" 1/2 N.M. Fd. Ambulance Condition excellent Shoeing not yet enough	
			" 1/3 N.M. Fd. Ambulance Very good	
	29/5/18		Inspected 4. 5.8 Coy. A.S.C. Good condition. Shoeing not good too much	
	30/5/18		ragging of wall	
	31/5/18		Inspected 452 Coy A.S.C. Condition improved. Shoeing not shoes	
			loose and feet broken.	

C. Hartley Major
D.A.D.V.S. 46th Div

Special WAR DIARY H.Q. (North Midland) Division
INTELLIGENCE (SUMMARY.) Page. 1.
(Erase heading not required.)

Summary of Events and Information

In accordance with Officer i/c., A.V.C. Base Records, No. 17/259/18 dated 12/5/18 & A.V.C. Records 85/WD/18, I have to furnish the following information with regard to the North Midland Division T.F. The information is given entirely from memory and is not to be looked on as, in any way, complete or even as being absolutely accurate. On leaving the Regular Army on 26th. September, 1913, I was gazetted to the Territorial Force with the rank of Temporary Lieut-Colonel in that Force and immediately took up the appointment of A.D.V.S., North Midland Division (T.F.). The Headquarters of this Division was at LICHFIELD, Staffordshire.

NORTH MIDLAND DIVISIONAL AREA, comprised the Counties of Stafford, Derby, Nottingham, Leicester, Rutland & Lincoln, & the Veterinary administration of the Units of the T.F. in those Counties came under me as A.D.V.S. I was the first A.D.V.S. to be appointed and prior to my appointment the Units were nominally under the Veterinary administration of the A.D.V.S., Northern Command, (York). In addition to the Units composing the North Midland Division, there were also two mounted Brigades located in the Area which also came under my Veterinary administration, viz:- The North Midland; & Notts. & Derby Mounted Brigades. (T.F.)

OFFICERS A.V.C./ & THE UNITS TO WHICH THEY WERE ATTACHED.

Major W.B.DICKENSON.-(Boston) attached 1st. N.M. Bde. (Lincolnshire) R.F.A.

Major J.W.GOE. (Stoke on Trent) attached 2nd.-N.M. Bde. (N.Staffordshire) R.F.A.

Lieut. M.T. SADLER. (Burton on Trent) attached 4th. N.M. Howitzer Bde. R.F.A.

Lieut. F.B.GRESHAM. (Newark on Trent) attached N.M. Divisional Train.

Captain J.A. CONNELL. (Lichfield) attached Staffordshire Yeomanry.

Captain T.H. HOBSON. (Leicester) attached Leicestershire Yeomanry.

Lieut. C. HARTLEY. (Lincoln) attached Lincolnshire Yeomanry.

Lieut. H.E. POWELL. (Coalville) attached Leicestershire R.H.A.

Special WAR DIARY 46th (North Midland) Division Army Form C. 2118.
or
INTELLIGENCE (SUMMARY). Page 2.
(Erase heading not required).

Stamp: OFFICER IN CHARGE RECORDS, 4 - JUN 19, ARMY VETERINARY C...

Place	Date	Hour	Summary of Events and Information	Remarks and references to Appendices
			Major E.D. JOHNSON. (Nottingham) attached South Notts. Hussars Yeomanry.	
			Lieut. R.M. AULTON. (Derby) attached Derbyshire Yeomanry.	
			Lieut. P.M. EVERSHED. (Nottingham) attached Nottinghamshire R.H.A.	
			OFFICERS A.V.C., (T.F.) RECRUITED PRIOR TO MOBILIZATION. I was only allowed to recruit Veterinary Surgeons resident within the Divisional Area, and the following were recruited :-	
			Lieut. T.V. BAGSHAW. Lieut. A.J. HINES. Lieut. J.A. SHAW. Lieut. W.G. THOMSON. Lieut. A.R. ROUTLEDGE; & Lieut. T. THOMSON having changed his residence from Shropshire to Staffordshire was transferred from the Welsh Division to the North Midland Division.	
			POSTING OF OFFICERS A.V.C., (T.F.) TO UNITS ON MOBILIZATION. A few days prior to the declaration of War secret orders were sent to each Officer informing him of the appointment he was to take up immediately mobilization was ordered, and the postings were as follows :-	
			O.C., N.M. Divisional Veterinary Hospital. Major J.W. COE.	
			Divisional Headquarters. Lieut. T.V. BAGSHAW.	
			Divisional R.E. Lieut. J.A. SHAW.	
			Divisional Train. Captain F.B. GRESHAM.	
			Lincolnshire Brigade R.F.A. (1st. North Midland.) Major W.B. DICKENSON. (This officer died a few days after the declaration of War.)	
			North Staffordshire Bde. R.F.A. (2nd. North Midland.) Lieut. W.G. THOMSON.	
			South Staffordshire Bde. R.F.A. (3rd. North Midland.) Lieut. T. THOMSON.	
			4th. N.M. Howitzer Bde. R.F.A. Lieut. M.T. SADLER.	

Army Form C. 2118.

Special WAR DIARY 46th (North Midland) Division
INTELLIGENCE SUMMARY. Page. 3.
(Erase heading not required.)

Summary of Events and Information

Lincoln & Leicester Infantry Bde.   Lieut. A.J.HINES.

MOUNTED BRIGADES:-

Staffordshire Yeomanry.   Captain J.A.CONNELL.   ⎫
Leicestershire Yeomanry.   Captain T.H.HOBSON.   ⎬ North Midland
Lincolnshire Yeomanry.   Captain G.HARTLEY.   ⎪ Mounted Brigade.
Leicestershire R.H.A.   Lieut. H.E.POWELL.   ⎭

South Notts. Hussars Yeomanry.   Major E.D.JOHNSON.   ⎫
Sherwood Rangers Yeomanry.   Lieut. A.R.ROUTLEDGE. ⎬ Notts. & Derby
Derbyshire Yeomanry.   Lieut. R.M.AULTON.   ⎪ Mounted Brigade.
Nottinghamshire R.H.A.   Lieut. P.M.EVERSHED. ⎭

The two Mounted Brigades ceased to be under the Veterinary administration of the A.D.V.S., North Midland Division immediately mobilization was ordered. So far as I remember, one additional Veterinary Officer was allowed on mobilization to each Mounted Brigade for duty with the Mounted Brigade Transport & Supply Column & Field Ambulance, but was not allowed on the peace establishments, and consequently was not recruited while those Brigades were under my Veterinary administration.

DATE OF MOBILIZATION. The North Midland Division, (T.F.) began to mobilize on the 4th. August, 1914. The Headquarters moved from LICHFIELD to DERBY on the 5th, August, 1914, and the Division was complete with horses & civilian transport within the specified number of days allowed for this in the "Mobilization Instructions." After about a week at Derby the Divisional Headquarters moved to LUTON in Bedfordshire, and all the Divisional Units were moved about the same time from the Derby Area to the LUTON Area.

Army Form C. 2118.

War Diary Special 46th North Midland Division

INTELLIGENCE (SUMMARY).   Page. 4.

(Erase heading not required.)

Place	Date	Hour	Summary of Events and Information	Remarks and references to Appendices
			CALL FOR OFFICERS, A.V.C. (T.F.) FOR SERVICE WITH THE REGULAR ARMY. The War Office wired for the names of officers of the A.V.C. (T.F.) who were willing to volunteer for service with the Regular A.V.C., and the following four officers of the North Midland Division were accepted within the first week of mobilization and at once proceeded to the Regular Units to which they were ordered :- Captain F.B.GRESHAM, Lieutenants M.T.SADLER, T.THOMSON & T.V.BAGSHAW. To replace those officers I obtained the services of the following Veterinary Surgeons who eventually got commissions in the A.V.C., (T.F.) :- J.R.CRANE, D.H.RYLANDS, H. NEWTON & H.C. TAYLOR.	
			NORTH MIDLAND DIVISIONAL VETERINARY HOSPITAL. The authority for the formation of this Unit was Army Order 66 dated War Office 1st, March, 1914. All the necessary arrangements for the formation of this Unit had been made prior to the date of mobilization. The Staffordshire T.F. Association had consented to take it under its administration, and Major J.W.COE had consented to become the Commanding Officer. Immediately War was declared, Major COE was instructed to at once recruit the authorized personnel in STOKE-ON-TRENT and this was done practically within the first 24 hours. The Territorial Force Association gave the O.C. permission to arrange locally for the clothing & equiping of the enlisted portion of the Personnel and this was practically completed within a fortnight. Major COE & the Personnel of the Veterinary Hospital were allowed to remain at STOKE-ON-TRENT until the 12th. August, 1914, so that the clothing & equiping of the men could be proceeded with as far as possible in that time. On the 12/8/14 they moved to DERBY and established a Veterinary Hospital in the Paddocks at the Race Course. The North Midland Divisional Veterinary Hospital remained at DERBY only a few days and was one of the last Units of the Division to move to the LUTON Area. While at DERBY it received the Mobilization Veterinary Equipment from the Army Veterinary Stores, WOOLWICH, and the Ordnance equipment was bought locally in DERBY by the D.A.D.O.S. of the Division. It was completely equiped both in respect of Veterinary & Ordnance equipment while at DERBY.	
			The Headquarters, Northern Command, had a scheme under which certain Veterinary Hospitals, which they called base Veterinary Hospitals, were to be established on mobilization at certain places in the Northern Command Area, and DERBY was one of those places, the others were, I think, DONCASTER & NEWCASTLE-ON-TYNE. I think it was unfortunate that this Base Veterinary Hospital scheme was not cancelled as soon as Army Order 66 dated War Office 1st. March, 1914, was published, as there was no need for those Base Hospitals after authority had been given for the formation of a Veterinary Hospital in each Territorial Division, and	

Army Form C. 2118.

Special WAR DIARY 46th North Midland Division
or
INTELLIGENCE SUMMARY.

Page 5.

(Erase heading not required.)

Place	Date	Hour	Summary of Events and Information	Remarks and references to Appendices

and so far as the one at DERBY was concerned, it was only a source of trouble and annoyance and never justified its existence. No equipment of any sort was apparently sanctioned for this Base Veterinary Hospital, and when the North Midland Division left DERBY the Headquarters, Northern Command, gave me direct orders that I was not to remove the Veterinary & Ordnance equipment which was at DERBY, and which belonged to the North Midland Veterinary Hospital, and that that equipment was to be left with the Base Veterinary Hospital. The result of this was that Major COE and the personnel had to proceed to LUTON with no Veterinary & Ordnance equipment. The Army Veterinary Stores & the D.A.D.O.S. refused to supply a second lot of equipment so that the personnel of the Divnl. V.H. were at LUTON for 10 days or a fortnight before I could obtain equipment and start the working of the V.H. and it was only then got as the result of the Divnl. Commander arranging for the supply when on a visit to the War Office. As soon as the equipment was received the North Midland Divnl. V.H. commenced to function as a Hospital and was located in STOCKWOOD PARK, LUTON.

About the 1st. September, 1914, the Headquarters, Northern Command, evidently came to the conclusion that the Base Veterinary Hospital at DERBY was not required, as it was abolished, and the personnel & equipment belonging to it was transferred to the North Midland Divnl. V.H. at LUTON. The Base V.H. at DERBY was directly under the administration of the A.D.V.S., Northern Command, and was not in any way connected with the North Midland Division. It was under the charge of a civilian Vety. Surgeon, Mr. A. SCOTSON. Amongst the personnel of the Base V.H. were 4 retired Farrier Quartermaster Sergeants, viz:- RUSSELL, HAZEL, NEWTON & one whose name I have forgotten, and those N.C.O's., as well as F.Q.M.S. SAUNDERS, late 5th. Lancers, who was already employed in the Divnl. V.H. at STOCKWOOD PARK, proved to be of the greatest value to the V.H. & to the Division.

Mobile Veterinary Sections. The first M.V.S. to be formed by the North Midland V.H. was named "B" M.V.S. and proceeded under the command of Lieut. D.H.RYLANDS, A.V.C. (T.F.) to join the South Midland Mounted Brigade sometime between the middle of September & the middle of October. The next one to be formed was the 1/1st. (N.M.) M.V.S. under the command of Captain C.HARTLEY, A.V.C., (T.F.) This Section was formed on the morning of the day the First Line North Midland Division left LUTON by route march for BISHOPS STORTFORD, which was sometime about the 20th. November, 1914, and has been a Unit of the Division ever since. Other M.V.S's. have been formed by the North Midland V.H. after it came under the administration of the Second Line North Midland Division, (now known as the 59th. Division.)

The North Midland V.H. remained under the Vety. administration of the A.D.V.S. North Midland Division (First Line) until that Division proceeded overseas in February, 1915,

WAR DIARY
INTELLIGENCE SUMMARY.

(Erase heading not required.)

Page. 6.

Place	Date	Hour	Summary of Events and Information	Remarks and references to Appendices
			when it came under the administration of the A.D.V.S., North Midland (Second Line) Division. Major J.W.COE. A.V.C. (T.F.) was appointed A.D.V.S., North Midland Division (Second Line) when that Division was formed & Lieut A.J.HINES A.V.C. (T.F.) was transferred from the First Line Division to command of the North Midland Divnl. V.H. In addition to the Officer Recruits already referred to the following Vety. Surgeons received commissions in the A.V.C. (T.F.) North Midland Division at LUTON :- G.G.SOOBY (Oakham); W.T.OLVER (Tamworth). The latter was transferred to the North Midland Mounted Brigade and Captain C.HARTLEY joined the North Midland Division in his place. The North Midland Division,(now known as the 46th. Division) remained in the BISHOP STORTFORD, SAFFRON WALDEN, BRAINTREE Area until February, 1915, when it proceeded to FRANCE. The Divnl. Headquarters left BISHOPS STORTFORD on 26th. February,1915, and disembarked at HAVRE on the last day of that month. After arrival in FRANCE the Division became known as the 46th. (North Midland) Division.	
			OFFICERS A.V.C. WHO CAME OVERSEAS WITH 46th. (NORTH MIDLAND) DIVISION.	
			Major (Temp. Lt.Colonel) W.A.McDOUGALL. A.D.V.S.	
			Captain C.HARTLEY. O.C.; 1/1st (N.M.)M.V.S.	
			Captain F.DOUTHWAITE. Attached 137th. Infantry Bde.	
			Lieut. J.A.SHAW. Attached 138th. Infantry Brigade.	
			Lieut. F.J.RICHMOND. Attached 139th. Infantry Brigade.	
			Lieut. H.C.TAYLOR. Attached 230th. Bde. R.F.A.	
			Lieut. W.G.THOMSON. Attached 231st. Bde. R.F.A.	
			Lieut. J.R.CRANE. Attached 232nd. Bde. R.F.A.	
			Lieut. H.NEWTON. Attached 4th. (N.M.) Howitzer Bde. R.F.A.	
			Lieut. J.FAGER. Attached 46th. Divnl. Ammunition Column.	
			Lieut. A.SCOTSON. Attached 46th. Divnl. Train.	
			Lieutenants J. FAGER & F.J.RICHMOND A.V.C. (T.F.) joined the 46th. (N.M.) Division from the East Anglian Division T.F. about 17th. February, 1915, in order to complete the Division in V.O's. owing to two Officers being transferred to Second Line. Captain F.DOUTHWAITE A.V.C. (T.F.) joined the Division with the Yorkshire Hussars Yeomanry, when that Regiment relieved the Northamptonshire Yeomanry, about October, 1914, as Divisional Cavalry. Only "B" Squadron, Yorkshire Hussars accompanied the Division overseas and Captain DOUTHWAITE was posted to the 137th. Infantry Bde. a few days before that Bde. embarked for FRANCE. Captain E.W.PARKS A.V.C. (T.F.) (Wellingborough) attached to the Northamptonshire Yeomanry also served with the 46th. (N.M.) Division	

Army Form C. 2118.

Special WAR DIARY
INTELLIGENCE SUMMARY

46th (Notts Midland) Division

Page 7.

(Erase heading not required.)

Instructions regarding War Diaries and Intelligence Summaries are contained in F. S. Regs., Part II. and the Staff Manual respectively. Title pages will be prepared in manuscript.

Place	Date	Hour	Summary of Events and Information	Remarks and references to Appendices
			during the time that Regiment was the Divisional Cavalry, viz:- From Mobilization until about October, 1914. Lieut. A.SCOTSON was invalided to ENGLAND in the spring of 1915, and Captain M.T.SADLER A.V.C. (T.F.) rejoined the Division on 1st. May, 1915, and remained with it until he was transferred to Home Service on 13th. October,1915. The number of Vety. Officers was reduced by four during October & November, 1915, and the following were transferred :- M.T.SADLER to ENGLAND; F.J.RICHMOND to 1st. Division; J.R.CRANE to Indian Vety. Hospital, ROUEN; & F.NEWTON to 50th. (Northumbrian) Division. Lieut. H.C.TAYLOR was evacuated sick on 8/8/15 & rejoined the Division on 6/10/15. He was again evacuated sick in the spring of 1916 and never rejoined the Division. Captain I.THOMSON A.V.C. (T.F.) was transferred from the Indian Cavalry to the 46th. Division to replace Lieut. H.C.TAYLOR and was attached to the 230th. Bde. R.F.A. When A.Ds.V.S. of Corps were first appointed in June, 1917, Lt. Colonel. W.A.McDOUGALL D.S.O., A.D.V.S., 46th. (N.M.) Division, was appointed A.D.V.S., I Corps from 21st. June, 1917, and Major C.HARTLEY, O.C., 1/1st.(N.M.) M.V.S. was appointed D.A.D.V.S., 46th. (N.M.) Division, and Captain J.PAGER was appointed O.C., 1/1st. (N.M.) M.V.S.	
Headquarter, I Corps.				
29th. May, 1918.				

W.M.McDougall
Lt. Colonel.
A.D.V.S., I Corps.
(Formerly A.D.V.S., 46th. (N.M.) Division.)

Army Form C. 2118.

WAR DIARY
or
INTELLIGENCE SUMMARY.
(Erase heading not required.)

DADVS 46th Div

June 1918

Place	Date	Hour	Summary of Events and Information	Remarks and references to Appendices
GOSWAY	1/6/18		Major C. HARTLEY A.V.C.(i) proceeded on leave to U.K. and CAPT T. THOMPSON A.V.C. took over his duties temporarily.	
	6/6/18		36 Remounts for Divisional Artillery inspected at D.A.C. Lines.	
	8/6/18		Inspected 27 Sheep sent up for Indian personnel of D.A.C.; had eleven of them slaughtered for Emaciation and Exhaustion and forwarded a report to the A.D.V.S.	
	10/6/18		Inspected Horses of the Division sent to the D.D.R's. casting parade.	
	14/6/18		Attended S.O.C.s inspection of Divisional Transport.	
	15.6.18		Major C HARTLEY A.V.C. returned from leave and resumed duties as D.A.D.V.S.	
	17/6/18		Inspected the N.M.M.V.S.	
	18.6.18		Received A.D.V.S. I copy – re application of Capt E DOUTHWAITE (A.V.C) application for transfer to home service.	
			Weekly meeting of V.O.'s	
	20.6.18		Attended conference of A.D.V.S. I copy.	
	22.6.18		Inspected 16th Dev Sy By R.E. Condition moderate. Grooming fair but has deteriorated.	
	24/6/18		Inspected B/231 Bde R.C.A. fair. C/231/Bde fair to good.	

WAR DIARY
or
INTELLIGENCE SUMMARY.
(Erase heading not required.)

Army Form C. 2118.

D.A.D.V.S. 46th Div.

June 1916

Place	Date	Hour	Summary of Events and Information	Remarks and references to Appendices
Gosnay	2.6.16		Visited 1/6th Battn. M.G.C.	
	3.6.16		Inspected 5th Sherwood Foresters — Good	
			" 6th Sherwood Foresters — Post to good. Unit relieving	
			" 466 (N.M.) Field Bde R.E. — Mules good. Horses fair	
			" 1st Monmouths. — Good. A much improved unit.	
			" 466 (N.M.) Field Coy R.E. — Mules satisfactory. Horses fair improving shortly	
			" 465 (N.M.) Field Coy R.E. — Mules satisfactory. Horses moderate to good	
			" 457 Coy A.S.C. — Good. Very short of men owing to sickness	
	4.6.16		Inspected 16 horses and mules of Bn H.Q 5th D.R.C. for transfer to remounts	
			All passed fit.	
	5.6.16		Inspected 4th Battery, 5th Army Bde R.F.A — Post to good. Field implements good	
			6th " " " " — "	
			D/5 " " " " — Good	
			Inspected animals put forward for casting for Remount returns	

Army Form C. 2118.

WAR DIARY
or
INTELLIGENCE SUMMARY.
(Erase heading not required.)

D.A.O.V.S. H.6th Div.

June 1918

Place	Date	Hour	Summary of Events and Information	Remarks and references to Appendices
Cosnay	22.6.18		Turnover transferred to XIII Corps. Lt. R. Gamble A.V.C to A.O.V.S.	
	30.6.18		Inspected 81st Battery 3rd Army Bgde R.F.A. Feet & good. Improved. 3rd Army B.A.C. Very good.	

E. Hartley
Major.
D.A.O.V.S.
H.6th Div.

Army Form C. 2118.

WAR DIARY
or
INTELLIGENCE SUMMARY.
(Erase heading not required.)

D.A.D.V.S. 46th Div.

July 1916

Instructions regarding War Diaries and Intelligence Summaries are contained in F. S. Regs., Part II. and the Staff Manual respectively. Title pages will be prepared in manuscript.

Place	Date	Hour	Summary of Events and Information	Remarks and references to Appendices
GOSNAY	4/7/16		Inspected 4th Battalion. M.G. Corps Mules good. Horses fair to good. Bad forge arrangements. Weekly meeting of V.O's.	
	5/7/16		Inspected A/230 Bgde. R.F.A. Satisfactory. B/230 Bgde R.F.A. Good. C/230 Bgde R.F.A. Fair to good. D/230 Bgde R.F.A. Fair. Capt. W.F. Thornton A.V.C. T.F. on 14 days leave to England.	
	6/7/16		D.D.V.S. 3rd Army inspected 1/1st N.M.M.K.S. Inspected 2nd N.M. Field Ambulance. Condition & grooming very good. Shoeing not good enough.	
	8/7/16		Inspected 137 Inf. Bgde. Condition and grooming very good. Shoeing not yet to standard. Too much dumping.	
	9/7/16		A.D.V.S. XIII Corps inspected 230 Bgde R.F.A. Inspected remounts before distribution.	
	10/7/16		Attended G.O.C's inspection of transport.	
	11/7/16		A.D.V.S. XIII Corps inspected 138 Inf. Bgde & 1st F.A.A. Section of 1st D.A.C. Inspected 44 remounts before distribution. Food class of I.O. Weekly meeting of V.O's.	

Army Form C. 2118.

WAR DIARY
or
INTELLIGENCE SUMMARY.
(Erase heading not required.)

D.A.D.V.S. 46th Div

July 1918.

Place	Date	Hour	Summary of Events and Information	Remarks and references to Appendices
COSNAY	13/7/18		O.D.R. 5th Army inspected cases for casting for remount returns.	
	15/7/18		No. S.E. 18768 Ofg/St. DIX, A.E. reported for duty with 46th Battalion M.G. Cps. No. S.E. 18768 Ofg/St. DIX, A.E. and gave cert in order to set him free from Quarantine for Epizootic Lymphangitis.	
	17/7/18		Inspected Section 1. 46th D.A.C. Section 1. 46th D.A.C. set free from three months quarantine. Attended L.O.C.'s transport inspection. Attended conference of A.D.V.S. XIII Corps with reference to clipping arrangements for ensuing winter.	
	18/7/18		Weekly meeting of V.O's.	
	19/7/18		A.D.V.S. XIII Corps inspected 91st Batty 8th Army Bde R.F.A, a case of Epizootic Lymphangitis having been diagnosed on L of C on horse cast down for destruction. Telluleted. Judged at 189 Inf. Bgde Horse Show. Judged at 46th Battalion M.G. Cops. Show. Capt. W.S. Thomson A.V.C. T.F.	
	24/7/18		returned from leave.	

Army Form C. 2118.

WAR DIARY
or
INTELLIGENCE SUMMARY.   D.A.D.V.S. #6th Div.

(Erase heading not required.)

Instructions regarding War Diaries and Intelligence Summaries are contained in F.S. Regs., Part II. and the Staff Manual respectively. Title pages will be prepared in manuscript.

Place	Date	Hour	Summary of Events and Information	Remarks and references to Appendices
Busnes	24.7.18		Attended A.D.C's Transport inspection	
	25.7.18		Inspected at 138 Inf. Bde. Horses	
	26.7.18		Weekly conference of V.O's	
	27.7.18		Inspected two horses for casting for remount reasons.	
			3rd Firing Bde. R.F.A. relieved by 46th Bde R.F.A (3rd Division)	
			V.O. y/c Capt. J. Thorneville A.V.C.	

C. Hunkey Major
D.A.D.V.S. #6th Div.

WR 37438
Army Form C2118

WAR DIARY
or
INTELLIGENCE SUMMARY
(Erase heading not required.)

D.A.D.V.S. 76th Div.

August 1918

Place	Date	Hour	Summary of Events and Information	Remarks and references to Appendices
COSNAY	1.8.18		Weekly meeting of V.O's. Captain R.A. Roberts A.V.C. (T.C.) reported for duty from No. 9 Veterinary Hospital. Divisional Horse Show.	
	2.8.18		Very heavy rain.	
	3.8.18		Inspected A/230 Bde. R.F.A. Condition of horses fair to good. D/230 Bde. R.F.A. Feet. In sheds on hardstand. Green. Floors needed improvement.	
	4.8.18		Judged at 1st Division Horse Show. D.D.V.S. 3rd Army inspected personnel my V.S. Capt. F. Douthwaite A.V.C. T.F. left for England to report to War Office for Home Service. Capt. R.A. Roberts A.V.C. (T.C.) took over his duties.	
	5.8.18		Inspected sick animals of 76th N.M. Field Ambulance. Also looked in for Eye male.	
	6.8.18		Inspected B/231 R.F.A. Horses good but have gone off slightly. Floor greasy and bad. C/231 R.F.A. Horses good. Have improved.	
	8.8.18		A.D.V.S. 7th Corps inspected 76th Battalion M.V.C. Weekly meeting of V.O's.	

Army Form C. 2118.

WAR DIARY
or
INTELLIGENCE SUMMARY.

D.A.D.V.S. 46th Div.

(Erase heading not required.)

August 1918

Instructions regarding War Diaries and Intelligence Summaries are contained in F. S. Regs., Part II. and the Staff Manual respectively. Title pages will be prepared in manuscript.

Place	Date	Hour	Summary of Events and Information	Remarks and references to Appendices
G.BS149	9.8.18		Inspected Section II. #61 D.A.C. in which a case of Mange had been discovered. Animals in good condition and clean. No more cases found.	
	12.8.18		XIII Corps Horse Show.	
	13.8.18		Inspected Section 1. #61 D.A.C. Horses good. Mules fair to good. D/231 Bde R.F.A. Condition good on the whole but about 10 horses on the light side. Grooming improved.	
			Inspected A/231 Bde R.F.A. Good.	
	15.8.18		Inspected 5th Sherwood Foresters. Very good.	
		6"	" Fair to good.	
		8"	" Good.	
			Weekly meeting of V.O's.	
	16.8.18		Inspected #61 Bde R.F.A. A Battery Condition & grooming good. Change fair B. Battery Condition of horses fair to good. Mules fair. Shoeing good	

(A7092) Wt. W12839/M1293 75,000. 1/17. D. D. & L., Ltd. Forms/C.2118/14.

Army Form C. 2118.

WAR DIARY
or
INTELLIGENCE SUMMARY.

D.A.D.V.S. 58th Div.

(Erase heading not required.)

August 1918

Place	Date	Hour	Summary of Events and Information	Remarks and references to Appendices
W.F. 18. GOSNAY.				
	10.8.18		C. Battery. Condition moderate. This unit has too many thin horses.	
	14.8.18		D. Battery. Condition good with exception of about 12 thin old horses. Shoeing fair. Saw mule feet too long.	
	18.8.18		Inspected at I Corps Horse Show.	
	19.8.18		Weekly meeting of V.O's.	
	23.8.18		Inspected 131 Inf. Bgde. Good throughout.	
	24.8.18		Inspected 18 horses and 10 mules which arrived for 1st Lovrain on 24th. All had lot in foot condition, shape, and 3 lame.	
	26.8.18		Inspected 138 Inf. Bgde. Good. Lot. 30 Lincoln Cyplus standard item to stop.	
	27.3.18 28.8.18		Inspected animals to shown to D.D.V.S. for 15/dog (9R2 - 16.1 O3 - 18 HD) The good. Not of weight tokin.	
	29.8.18.		Inspected 1st Monmouth. Condition good except 3 remounts.	
	30.8.18		#52 Coy R.S.C. Condition improved. #53 Coy A.S.C. Condition good. Shoeing fair.	

WAR DIARY
or
INTELLIGENCE SUMMARY.

Army Form C. 2118.

WO 40

D.A.D.V.S. 46th Div.

September 1918

Place	Date	Hour	Summary of Events and Information	Remarks and references to Appendices
Cosnay	2.9.18		A.D.V.S. XIII Corps inspected 46th Div. from A.S.R.S.	
	3.9.18		Inspected 46th Div. Sig. Co. R.E. Condition poor to good. Too many thin horses. Evening feed. Shoeing good.	
	4.9.18		A.D.V.S. XIII Corps inspected 231 Bde R.F.A. A Battery horses in good condition. B Battery very good. C Battery good, but then horses not seen. D Battery improving especially in grooming. Grooming and shoeing satisfactory throughout. Infected animals for evacuation at M.V.S.	
	5.9.18		Weekly meeting of V.O's.	
	6.9.18		46th Bde R.F.A. leaves 46th Div. and passes to 9th Division for Veterinary Administration.	

Army Form C. 2118.

WAR DIARY
or
INTELLIGENCE SUMMARY.
(Erase heading not required.)

D.A.D.V.S. 46th Div.

September 1918

Place	Date	Hour	Summary of Events and Information	Remarks and references to Appendices
GOSNAY	1918			
	7.9.18		Inspected 230 Bde. R.F.A at HESDIGNEUL.	
			A/230 Battery. Condition poor. Good. Too many thin horses. Grooming fair.	
			B. Battery. Condition good. Grooming not good at the moment.	
			C. " " Fair to good. Improved. Grooming good.	
			D. " " Fair to good. Horses light but hard and clean.	
	8.9.18		Capt. John Faust A.V.C. T.F admitted to 1/1st N.M.F.A. Bullers with P.U.O.	
			Capt. T. Thomson takes over command of 1/1st N.M.V.R.	
	9.9.18		Visited 138 Inf. Bde., S.A.A Section, #6th D.A.C. & #6th Battalion M.G.C.	
			Attended D.D.V.R.'s Cantin, Hamel.	
	10.9.18		A.D.V.S. xxII Corps inspected 460 (N.M.) Fld. Coy. R.E. Very good.	
			" #6th Battalion M.G.C. Satisfactory.	

WAR DIARY
or
INTELLIGENCE SUMMARY.

Army Form C. 2118.

September 1918.   D.A.D.V.S. 46th Div.

Place	Date	Hour	Summary of Events and Information	Remarks and references to Appendices
GOSNAY	12.9.18		Division moved by train to BEAUCOURT Area. Very few casualties.	
BEAUCOURT and LA HAIRIE	14.9.18		Joined III Corps. Visited A.D.V.S. III Corps at CANNOY. Inspected 48th Battn M.G. Corps at BAIZIEUX. All in fat good cover. Condition fair to good. Grooming good.	
	15.9.18		Visited 1/1st N.M.M.V.S. at HEILLY. Capt. J. FACER A.V.C. T.F. returned from hospital and resumed command of Section. Capt. T. Thomson A.V.C. T.F. returned to 230 Bgde R.F.A.	
	16.9.18		Visited 465 (N.M.) Field Coy R.E. - 1st Monmouths - 3rd Sherwood Foresters - 2nd Sherwood Foresters - 21 Q.A.H.C. - 2nd Life Guards. Glou. Battery detached to 12th ult Division.	
	17.9.18		Inspected sick horses at M.V.S.	
TERTRY	19.9.18		Division moved to COURCY Farm, TERTRY, and joined IX Corps. The transport took two days to march and stood it well that there were a few sore shoulders.	
	20.9.18		Visited MONS-EN-CHAUSSEE and billeted M.V.S. in excellent place at sugar factory.	
VRAIGNES	21.9.18		Division moved to VRAIGNES. Attended conference of A.D.V.S. IX Corps.	

Army Form C. 2118.

WAR DIARY
or
INTELLIGENCE SUMMARY.
(Erase heading not required.)

D.A.D.V.S. 46th Div.

September 1918

Place	Date	Hour	Summary of Events and Information	Remarks and references to Appendices
VRAIGNES	22.9.18		Visited 6th & 8th Sherwood Foresters & 5th Lincolns at VENDELLES & BERNES.	
	23.9.18		Had been shelled during night. 26 Casualties.	
			Inspected horses for evacuation at M.V.S.	
	24.9.18		Visited 466th Batton M.G. Corps & 466 (W.M) Field Coy R.E. Our Artillery scene	
	25.9.18		Visited Artillery. Horses have lost a good deal of flesh but looked fit and are standing work well. Had several cases of Dermatitis of Heels due to Mustard Gas. Capt K.O. Roberts A.V.C. goes on leave.	
	26.9.18		Advanced post of M.V.S. established at Q.13. d. 4. 3. Sheet 62 c.	
	29.9.18		Weekly meeting of V.O.'s	
	30.9.18		Visited 216 A.T. (Ay R.E.) 180 T (By R.E.) #65 (Army) Field Coy R.E. 231 Bde R.F.A	

C. Hartley
Major A.V.C. T.F.

Army Form C. 2118.

WAR DIARY
or
INTELLIGENCE SUMMARY.
(Erase heading not required.)

D.A.D.V.S. 46th Div.
October 1918

Instructions regarding War Diaries and Intelligence Summaries are contained in F.S. Regs., Part II. and the Staff Manual respectively. Title pages will be prepared in manuscript.

Place	Date	Hour	Summary of Events and Information	Remarks and references to Appendices
VRAIGNES	1st		Inspected animals for evacuation at M.V.S.	
	2nd		Inspected Section 1. 46 D.A.C. Satisfactory. Section 11. Satisfactory except evacuation.	
R.I.S.B.B.	3rd		Weekly meeting of V.O's. Moved to R.I.S.B.B. West 62.C.	
VENDELLES	5th		Attended conference of A.D.V.S. IX Corps. Advanced post of M.V.S. at R.6.c.35. Shelters.	
	6th		Inspected 3rd Sherwoods - Good. 6th Sherwoods Fair. 8th Sherwoods Fair.	
	7th		Inspected 126 remounts. 8.R. Bar and small. 4 Pack. Fair. 57 L.D. Fair. 20 Mules. Good - 30 H.D. Good. Inspected 1/2 and 1/3 N.M. Field Ambulance. Very good. 466 (N.M.) Field Coy R.E. Satisfactory - 466 (N.M.) Field Coy R.E. Moderate. Some thin horses.	
	8th		Inspected animals for evacuation at M.V.S.	
	9th		Inspected 231 Bgde. R.F.A. Horses going down but on the whole satisfactory. Moved to FRESNOY.	
FRESNOY	10th			
	11th		Weekly meeting of V.O's. Captain H. Roberts A.V.C. returned from leave.	

Army Form C. 2118.

WAR DIARY
or
INTELLIGENCE SUMMARY.
(Erase heading not required.)

D.A.D.V.S. 46th Div.

October 1918

Place	Date	Hour	Summary of Events and Information	Remarks and references to Appendices
FRESNOY	12th		Visited Sig Coy R.E. One section very dirty but the management is improving and the rest is trying hard. C Company 466th Bat'n M.G.C. Animals tired and foot especially the horses. C/230 Bde R.F.A. Horse that condition but horses are bright and will do a lot more work.	
	13th		Visited 1/1st & 1/2nd N.M. Fd Ambulances. Good. 465 (N.M.) Field Coy R.E. Fair. Some manes want hogging and more grooming is required. Visited Sections 1 & 11 46th DAC	
	14th		Capt. T. Thomson A.V.C. T.F. on leave to England. Inspected horses for evacuation at M.V.S. Two horses of 1/5 Leicesters badly blistered from Mustard gas. Inspected 466 (N.M.) Field Coy R.E. Improving but too closely packed in stables. Ordered day line. 1st Monmouths. Good except one horse. 1/5th Leicesters In good stables. Mules good. Horse foot.	
	15th		100 L.D. remounts for Div. Artillery inspected by Capt W.G. Thomson. He reported favourably.	

Army Form C. 2118.

WAR DIARY
or
INTELLIGENCE SUMMARY.
(Erase heading not required.)

D.A.D.V.S. 46th Div.

October 1918.

Instructions regarding War Diaries and Intelligence Summaries are contained in F.S. Regs., Part II. and the Staff Manual respectively. Title pages will be prepared in manuscript.

Place	Date	Hour	Summary of Events and Information	Remarks and references to Appendices
FRESNOY	16th		Inspected 48 remounts at lines of 451 By. R.S.L.P. 32 R. Poor except 2 off. 6 Both Feet	
			10 A.D. Fair. Killed B/230 Bgde. R.F.A at FRESNOY. Foot condition but still good.	
	17th		Weekly meeting of V.O's.	
	18th		Inspected sick animals for evacuation at M.V.S.	
	20th		Went to find a derelict horse on BOMAIN-AISONVILLE Rd. Ordered flesh to collect.	
	21st		Inspected A/230 Bgde R.F.A. In fair. Horses thin but hard.	
			at G/230 Bgde R.F.A. Under cover. Horses hold in condition but efficient.	
			BOMAIN Only four or five there.	
			D/230 Bgde R.F.A. Have lost a lot of condition and have too many thin horses	
	23rd		Inspected 454 Coy A.S.C. In open near GOUY-HART. Horses rough but in good condition	
			452 Coy A.S.C. " " In hard condition but on light side.	
			453 Coy A.S.C. " " Good.	
			3rd (N.M.) Field Ambulance In stables at FRESNOY. Much too warm.	
			Inspected a stray horse In very good condition. Inspected horses for evacuation at M.V.S.	

Army Form C. 2118.

WAR DIARY
or
INTELLIGENCE SUMMARY.
(Erase heading not required.)

October 1918. D.A.O.V.S. 46th Div.

Place	Date	Hour	Summary of Events and Information	Remarks and references to Appendices
FRESNOY.	24th		Inspected 1/5th Sherwoods at FRESNOY. Much satisfactory. Horses have lost condition. Stables very dirty.	
			1/6th Sherwood Foresters. Generals clean and hard but come too thin.	
			Weekly Meeting of V.O's.	
	25th		Inspected B/231 Bgde R.F.A. Horses thin but bright need rest tally.	
			" A/231 " R.F.A. Too many thin horses which want much grooming and attention.	
			" C/231 " R.F.A. In fair condition.	
			" B/231 " R.F.A. Satisfactory. The best unit in the Brigade.	
	26th		" Section 1. 46th D.A.C. in open at BEAUREGARD Farm. Have lost condition but are on the whole satisfactory.	
			Inspected Section II. Going off especially E sub. Too many front galls.	
	27th		Inspected the Divl Mounted Troop. Cart horses in use and reported that too should be changed as unsuitable for the work.	

Army Form C. 2118.

WAR DIARY
or
INTELLIGENCE SUMMARY.
(Erase heading not required)

D.A.D.V.S. 46th Div.

October 1918.

Place	Date	Hour	Summary of Events and Information	Remarks and references to Appendices
FRESNOY.	27th		Pte/Sgt Cochrane E. reported for duty and posted to 46th Battn. M.G.C. Inspected animals for evacuation at M.V.S.	
	28th		Visited 138 Inf. Bgde. Examined Pte's Hough & Barton 1/6 Nth Staffs Regt as shoeing smiths. Hough failed, Barton passed.	
	29th		Inspected 46th Battalion M.G. Corps. All improving especially B & D Coys.	
	30th		Visited office of D.A.D.V.S. 32nd Div. & 42 M.V.S. Inspected animals of 907 Labour Coy. All well but two intermit horses which were thin & tired.	
BOHAIN	31st		Moved to BOHAIN.	

C. Hartley
Major AVC T.F.

17/v

WAR DIARY
or
INTELLIGENCE SUMMARY
(Erase heading not required.)

Army Form C. 2118.

D.A.D.V.S. 46th Div.

November 1918

Place	Date	Hour	Summary of Events and Information	Remarks and references to Appendices
BOHAIN	1st		Weekly meeting of V.O's.	
	2nd		Visited A.D.V.S. 1st Corps at BUSIGNY. Visited 1/2nd & 1/3rd N.M. Field Ambulances and 138 Inf. Bde. 1 Capt. T. Thomson A.V.C.F. returned from leave. All well.	
	3rd		Inspected animals for evacuation at PRISCHES. Inspected A/230 Bde R.F.A. Poor. B/230 Bde R.F.A. Fair. D/230 Bde. Poor and going off. Section 1. 46th D.A.C. Satisfactory. Section 11. 46th D.A.C. Improving but not as good as they should be. Sgt. A.E. Dix A.V.C. returned from leave and posted to Section 1. 46th D.A.C. Moved to MOLAIN.	
MOLAIN	5th		Visited 466 N.M. Field Coy R.E. Animals poor. 468 N.M. Field Coy R.E. & 1st Monmouths. Satisfactory. Moved to CATILLON.	
CATILLON	6th		Inspected and evacuated 84 remounts. Robert Mules and Pack Pair. A.D. V.D Post. A batch of 74 for On Rly over 8 days good.	

(A7092) Wt W12859/M1293. 75,500. 4/17. D. D. & L., Ltd. Forms/C.2118/14.

Army Form C. 2118.

WAR DIARY
or
INTELLIGENCE SUMMARY.

(Erase heading not required.)

D.A.D.V.S. 46th Div.

November 1918.

Instructions regarding War Diaries and Intelligence Summaries are contained in F. S. Regs., Part II. and the Staff Manual respectively. Title pages will be prepared in manuscript.

Place	Date	Hour	Summary of Events and Information	Remarks and references to Appendices
PRISCHES	8th		Moved to PRISCHES and established an advanced post of D.V.S. there	
			Inspected D/230 Bde R.F.A. Horses thin and there are several debilitated horses to be sent away. Rear part of B/230 Bde & C/230 Bde which are satisfactory.	
	9th		Visited S.A.A. Section 46th D.A.C. Very good. A.D.V.S. IX Corps called and arranged staging stations to V.E.S.	
	10th		Inspected animals for evacuation at M.V.S.	
SAINS DU NORD	11th		Moved to SAINS-DU-NORD.	
	12th		Inspected Signal Coy R.E., 5th Leicester & B.Coy 46th Battn M.G.C. Satisfactory	
LANDRECIES	14th		Moved to LANDRECIES.	
	15th		Inspected animals at 4/1st N.M.V.S.	
	16th		Inspected 46 animals for transfer to 1st Division. Infected animals for evacuation at 4/1st N.M.V.S.	

Army Form C. 2118.

WAR DIARY
or
INTELLIGENCE SUMMARY.
(Erase heading not required.)

Army Form C. 2118.

D.A.D.V.S.   46th Division

November 1918

Place	Date	Hour	Summary of Events and Information	Remarks and references to Appendices
Landrecies	17th		CAPT. ROBERTS inspected 104 F.D. for transfer to IX Corps	
	18th		MAJOR C. HARTLEY proceeded on leave. CAPT.T.THOMSON, A.V.C, F.F. took over duties of D.A.D.V.S.	
	21st		Inspected 80 Remounts; 50 L.D. & 30 Mules; L.Ds. poor and skin very dirty, Mules fair	
	24th		Inspected 50 Remounts; 30 L.D. & 20 Mules received from VIII Corps V.E.S. The horses were in poor condition and an inferior lot; the mules were fairly good.	
	29th		Attended Divisional Conference when the clipping of horses was discussed. It was decided to try and obtain permission to clip all draught animals trace high as well as all Riding horses in view of the altered conditions of working.	

J. Thomson
Capt. A.V.C. (F.F.)
D.A.D.V.S. 46th Division

Army Form C. 2118.

WAR DIARY
or
INTELLIGENCE SUMMARY.
(Erase heading not required.)

O.A.D.V.S. H.Qrs. 66

December 1918.

Place	Date	Hour	Summary of Events and Information	Remarks and references to Appendices
LANDRECIES	3rd		Capt W.L. THOMSON R.A.V.C. T.F. granted 14 days special leave to England.	
	5th		Major C. HARTLEY R.A.V.C. T.F. returned from leave and resumed duties as D.A.D.V.S.	
	6th		Sgt. KEMP R.A.V.C. attached 139 Inf. Bgde granted 14 days special leave to England	
	11th		137 Inf Bgde, 1/3rd N.M. Field Ambulance & 453 Coy R.A.S.C. moved to FRESNOY-LE-GRAND & 46th Battn M.G.C. to BOHAIN. Capt H.A. ABBOTT R.A.V.C. sent in vety charge of these units.	
	12th		Weekly meeting of V.O.'s. Instructions received to inspect all animals to ascertain and select those suitable for tracking. Board to consist of Lt. Col. L. PHIPPS 17th Monmouths. Capt. PHIPPS BERKELEY Horsemaster to 231 Bgde R.F.A. and myself.	
	15th		Inspected animals of Capt E. Abot #65 - #66 and #68 Army Fd. Bgde R.E.	
	17th		Inspected all animals of 66th Div. Artillery.	

WAR DIARY
or
INTELLIGENCE SUMMARY.

Army Form C. 2118.

D.A.D.V.S. 61st (N.M.) Division

December 1916.

Place	Date	Hour	Summary of Events and Information	Remarks and references to Appendices
LANDRECIES	18th		Inspected mares of 1/6th D.H.Q., 7 & 8th Div Sig. By R.E., 139 Inf Bgde, 138 Inf Bgde.	
	19th		1st and 1/2nd N.M. Field Ambulances & 1/1st Monmouth Bgt.	
			Inspected mares of 137 Inf Bgde & 46th Battalion M.G. Corps & 1/3 N.M. Field Ambulance.	
			Weekly meeting of V.O.'s.	
	20th		Inspection committee of XIII Corps inspected the selected mares at 1/1st N.M. Mobile Vety Section. Six mares were branded on left cheek only.	
	23rd		Inspected R.E. units at PREUX.	
	24th		In accordance with instructions contained in G/1/30 of 20.12.16 of I.G.V.S. the classification of animals of the division was commenced.	
			1/230 Bgde RFA was classified.	
	28th		Classified the animals of 139 Inf Bgde.	

Army Form C. 2118.

WAR DIARY
or
INTELLIGENCE-SUMMARY.

(Erase heading not required.)

D.A.D.V.S. 46th Div.

December 1918

Place	Date	Hour	Summary of Events and Information	Remarks and references to Appendices
LANDRECIES	30th		Inspected Section 1 & 11 46th D.A.C.	
	31st		Inspected Band C/230 Bde R.F.A. & B/231 Bde R.F.A.	

C. Hartley
Major D.A.D.V.S.
46th Div.

Army Form C. 2118.

WAR DIARY
or
INTELLIGENCE SUMMARY.
(Erase heading not required.)

D.A.D.V.S. 46th Div.

January 1919

Place	Date	Hour	Summary of Events and Information	Remarks and references to Appendices
LANDRECIES	1st		Classified animals of C.R.E. Hdqrs, 465-466-468 (N.M.) Field Coys. R.E. and #62 Coy. R.S.C.	
	2nd		Classified #57 Coy A.S.C. - 46th Div. Sig. Coy R.E. v M.M.P. Weekly meeting of V.O's.	
	3rd		Classified A/231 v C/231 Bgde R.F.A and A/230 Bgde R.F.A v 230 Bgde Hdqrs	
	4th		Classified D/231 Bgde R.F.A v 461 Coy R.S.C.	
	6th		Classified 136 Inf Bgde - 1/2 N.M. F.A Ambulance and West Mounted.	
	7th		" 139 Inf Bgde - 463 Coy A.S.C. and 1/3rd N.M. F.A Ambulance	
	8th		" 46th Battalion M.G.C.	
	9th		Moved to LE CATEAU.	
LE CATEAU	10th		Classified C.R.A Hdqrs - 231 Bgde Hdqrs - S.A.A. Section, 463 S.A.C	

Army Form C. 2118.

WAR DIARY
or
INTELLIGENCE SUMMARY.

(Erase heading not required.)

J.A.D.V.S. 46th Div

January 1919

Place	Date	Hour	Summary of Events and Information	Remarks and references to Appendices
LE CATEAU	11th		Visited POMMEREUIL and inspected stabling suggested of Mayor infection with a view to their disinfection.	
	15th		Visited 138 Inf. Bgde.	
	16th		Visited Y & Z animals of 1/6th Leicesters, 1/5th Lincolns	
			" " 138 Inf Bgde HdQrs, 1/4th Leicesters, 1/5th Lincolns	
	20th		" 1st Monmouths.	
	21st		Visited Y & Z animals of 452 Coy A.S.C. and inspected animals of above	
	22nd		" " 46th D.H.Q. and inspected 452 Coy A.S.C.	
	24th		" " 46th Div Sig Coy R.E.	
	26th		Visited 1/1st N.M.M.V.S.	
	27		Inspected 200 Y horses for demobilisation	

Army Form C. 2118.

WAR DIARY
or
INTELLIGENCE SUMMARY.

(Erase heading not required.)

D.A.D.V.S. 46th Div.

January 1919

Place	Date	Hour	Summary of Events and Information	Remarks and references to Appendices
LE CATEAU	29th		Visited all units of Division with Capt Bevors-Kircher M.C. the acting D.A.D.R. to inspect & reclassify the remaining Y. horses.	
	31st		Inspected 150 Y horses for demobilisation	

C. Hartley Major
D.A.D.V.S. 46th Div.

Army Form C. 2118.

WAR DIARY
or
INTELLIGENCE SUMMARY.
(Erase heading not required.)

D.A.O.V.S. 46th Div.

February 1919

Place	Date	Hour	Summary of Events and Information	Remarks and references to Appendices
LE CATEAU	1st		Capt. J. Facet R.A.V.C. T.F. proceeded on 14 days leave to England.	
	2nd to 7th		Capt. T. Thomson R.A.V.C. T.F. takes over command of 1/1st M.M.V.S. Killed all units of division with D.A.D.R. to re-classify animals	
	8th		Inspected 48 Y animals of 46th Div. drawn before demobilisation	
	10th		Inspected 30 Z animals sent to Paris for sale	
	12 & 13th		Selected 100 animals for dispersal sale at LE CATEAU	
	14th		Capt. J. Facet granted 14 days extension of leave	
	15th		Dispersal sale at LE CATEAU. 90 horses average Fr 8.80 — 10 mules average Fr 397	
	19th & 20th		Selected 100 animals for dispersal sale at LE CATEAU. 100 for sale at BOHAIN	
	20th		1/1st N.M.M.V.S. moved to LE CATEAU. Took over command for Capt. T. Thomson	
	22nd		Dispersal sale at LE CATEAU. 80 horses average Fr 1020 — 20 mules average Fr 24st	
	24th		Dispersal sale at BOHAIN which was arranged by XIII Corps. Sale stopped by order of A.D.V.S. when 38 animals had been sold. Average = 26 horses Fr 651, 12 mules Fr 481.	

Army Form C. 2118.

WAR DIARY
or
INTELLIGENCE SUMMARY.
(Erase heading not required.)

D.A.D.V.S. 76th Div.

February 1919

Place	Date	Hour	Summary of Events and Information	Remarks and references to Appendices
LE CATEAU	23rd		Inspected 282 horses for despatch to Paris & 12 Riders for despatch to Havre.	
	28th		Dispatched mules at PRISCHES. 55 horses averaged frs 1090 - 41 mules average frs 617	
	27th & 28th		Selected 156 animals for sale at LE CATEAU.	

C. Hartley Major
D.A.D.V.S. 76th Div.

D.A.D.V.S. 76th Div.

Army Form C. 2118.

WAR DIARY
or
INTELLIGENCE SUMMARY.
(Erase heading not required.)

D.A.D.V.S. 46th Dist.

March 1919

Instructions regarding War Diaries and Intelligence Summaries are contained in F. S. Regs., Part II. and the Staff Manual respectively. Title pages will be prepared in manuscript.

Place	Date	Hour	Summary of Events and Information	Remarks and references to Appendices
LE CATEAU	1st		Deferred sale at LE CATEAU. 116 horses averaged Fr.1104 - 30 mules averaged Fr.617	
	2nd		Inspected 50 7 mules for shipment at Caudry Station.	
	3rd		Selected animals from 230 Bgde R.F.A. v D.A.C. for sale	
	5th		Deferred sale at LANDRECIES. 93 horses at Fr.730 - 28 mules at Fr.534	
	6th		Selected animals from 230 Bgde R.F.A. v D.A.C. for sale	
	8th		Deferred sale at LE CATEAU. 82 horses at Fr.755 - 33 mules at Fr.495	
	9th		Selected animals from 231 Bgde #6th Div from 20 for sale	
	12th		Deferred sale at PRISCHES. 94 horses averaged 928 fr. 2 mules at Fr.575.	
	15th		Capt. R. A. Roberts R.A.V.C. left for demobilization.	
	31st		There is nothing particular to report for the rest of the month. The demobilization of A.V.C. personnel commenced at the division area. Brought down to Cadre A. Major Carther Capt. T. Thomson v Capt. J. G. Thomson left for demobilization.	

www.ingramcontent.com/pod-product-compliance
Lightning Source LLC
Chambersburg PA
CBHW082007220426
43670CB00014B/2571